PRESENT PASTS

Cultural Memory
in
the
Present

Mieke Bal and Hent de Vries, Editors

PRESENT PASTS

Urban Palimpsests and the Politics of Memory

Andreas Huyssen

STANFORD UNIVERSITY PRESS

STANFORD, CALIFORNIA

Stanford University Press
Stanford, California

Several of the essays in this book appeared in earlier versions:
Chapter 1. "Present Pasts: Media, Politics, Amnesia," *Public Culture,* special issue on globalization, 12, no. 1 (2000): 21–38.
Chapter 2. "Monumental Seduction," *New German Critique* 69 (Fall 1996): 181–200.
Chapter 3. "The Voids of Berlin," *Critical Inquiry* 24, no. 1 (Autumn 1997): 57–81.
Chapter 4. "After the War: Berlin as Palimpsest," *Harvard Design Magazine* (Spring 2000): 70–75.
Chapter 5. "Fear of Mice: The Transformations of Times Square," *Harvard Design Magazine* (Winter/Spring 1998): 26–28.
Chapter 7. "Unland: The Orphan's Tunic," in Nancy Princenthal et al., *Doris Salcedo* (London: Phaidon, 2000), 90–103.
Chapter 8. "Of Mice and Mimesis: Reading Spiegelman with Adorno," *New German Critique* 81 (Fall 2000): 65–82.
Chapter 10. "Twin Memories: Afterimages of Nine/Eleven," *Grey Room* 7 (Spring 2002): 8–13.

Printed in the United States of America on acid-free, archival-quality paper.

Library of Congress Cataloging-in-Publication Data

Huyssen, Andreas.
    Present pasts : urban palimpsests and the politics of memory /Andreas Huyssen.
        p.   cm.—(Cultural memory in the present)
    Includes bibliographical references.
    ISBN 0-8047-4560-9 (cloth : alk. paper)—ISBN 0-8047-4561-7 (pbk. : alk. paper)
    1. Memory (Philosophy)   2. History—Philosophy.   3. Memory—Social aspects.
4. Cities and towns—Psychological aspects.   5. Memory in literature.
I. Title.   II. Series.
BD181.7.H89   2003
901—dc21   2002007737

Original Printing 2003

Last figure below indicates year of this printing:
12   11

Typeset by Heather Boone in 11/13.5 Garamond

For Nina, again

Contents

Illustrations

Even now, when I try to remember . . . , the darkness does not lift but becomes yet heavier as I think how little we can hold in mind, how everything is constantly lapsing into oblivion with every extinguished life, how the world is, as it were, draining itself, in that the history of countless places and objects which themselves have no power of memory is never heard, never described or passed on.

—W. G. SEBALD, *Austerlitz,* p. 24

Introduction

The Crisis of History

Historical memory today is not what it used to be. It used to mark the relation of a community or a nation to its past, but the boundary between past and present used to be stronger and more stable than it appears to be today. Untold recent and not so recent pasts impinge upon the present through modern media of reproduction like photography, film, recorded music, and the Internet, as well as through the explosion of historical scholarship and an ever more voracious museal culture. The past has become part of the present in ways simply unimaginable in earlier centuries. As a result, temporal boundaries have weakened just as the experiential dimension of space has shrunk as a result of modern means of transportation and communication.

In times not so very long ago, the discourse of history was there to guarantee the relative stability of the past in its pastness. Traditions, even though themselves often invented or constructed and always based on selections and exclusions, gave shape to cultural and social life. Built urban space—replete with monuments and museums, palaces, public spaces, and government buildings—represented the material traces of the historical past in the present. But history was also the mise-en-scène of modernity. One learned from history. That was the assumption. For about two centuries, history in the West was quite successful in its project to anchor the ever more transitory present of modernity and the nation in a multifaceted but strong narrative of historical time. Memory, on the other hand, was a topic for the poets and their visions of a golden age or, conversely, for their tales about the hauntings of a restless past. Literature was of course valued highly as part of the national heritage constructed to mediate religious, ethnic, and class conflicts within a nation. But the main concern of the nineteenth-century nation-states was to mobilize and monumentalize national and universal pasts so as to legitimize and give meaning to the present and to envision the future: culturally, politically, socially. This model no longer works. Whatever the specific content of the many contemporary debates about history and memory may be, underlying them is a fundamental disturbance not just of the relationship between history as objective and scientific, and memory as subjective and personal, but of history itself and its promises. At stake in the current history/memory debate is not only a disturbance of our notions of the past, but a fundamental crisis in our imagination of alternative futures.

For it was really the future that captured the imagination of post-Enlightenment Europe and the United States after independence. In the wake of the eighteenth-century revolutions and the secular imagination they unleashed, the spaces of utopia, rather static and confined since Thomas More, were increasingly temporalized and set in motion, and the road to utopia became fair game for a worldly historical imagination. Progress and historical teleologies were embraced across much of the political spectrum, but this inevitably meant shedding the past. The price paid for progress was the destruction of past ways of living and being in the world. There was no liberation without active destruction. And the destruction of the past brought forgetting. From the beginning, modernity was Janus-faced in its negotiations of cultural memory. The Romantic lament about a world lost under the onslaught of industrialization, urbanization, and modernity only goes to show how fast and intense the transformations toward the future had already become by 1800. The other side of this loss was what Nietzsche, in his *Untimely Meditations*, called the nineteenth century's hypertrophy of history, which he countered with his seductive call for creative forgetting.

The Hypertrophy of Memory

Today, we seem to suffer from a hypertrophy of memory, not history. It is not always clear what is at stake in this semantic shift, and the intense recent debates about history vs. memory have only rarely carried us beyond entrenched professional or political interests. But there is agreement that the playing field has been radically altered. The question is about whether the change is for better or for worse, and there seems to be an overriding desire to decide one way or the other.

Of course, memory is one of those elusive topics we all think we have a handle on. But as soon as we try to define it, it starts slipping and sliding, eluding attempts to grasp it either culturally, sociologically, or scientifically. After more than a decade of intense public and academic discussions of the uses and abuses of memory, many feel that the topic has been exhausted. Memory fatigue has set in. Although I would agree with a certain sense of excess and saturation in the marketing of memory, I think that the call simply to move on risks forfeiting what the recent convulsions of memory discourse have generated. Directed against the culture industry's exploitation of hot themes and popular topics, the call to forget memory just reproduces the industry's own fast-paced mechanism of declaring obsolescence. And it fails to give us a plausible explanation for the obsession with memory itself as a significant symptom of our cultural present. The first essay of this book attempts instead to suggest an historical explanation of contemporary memory culture and its politics.

Memory used to be associated either with canonical traditions or with the structures of rhetoric that were considered absolutely essential to make social and cultural memory possible. Since Romanticism and the decline of the rhetorical traditions, memory was increasingly associated with ideas of experience and its loss. Readers of Wordsworth's *Prelude* or of Proust's *A la recherche du temps perdu* are well versed in the bittersweet tunes of memory. But neither Wordsworth nor Proust was compelled to think about memory and forgetting as social and political issues of global proportions, as we are today. If the Romantics thought that memory bound us in some deep sense to times past, with melancholia being one of its liminal manifestations, then today we rather think of memory as a mode of re-presentation and as belonging ever more to the present. After all, the act of remembering is always in and of the present, while its referent is of the past and thus absent. Inevitably, every act of memory carries with it a dimension of betrayal, forgetting, and absence. This is what the epistemological discourse of constructivism, which in its legitimate critique of the naturalization of tradition and nation often overshoots its mark, ultimately and correctly implies.

Thinking about memory in this way makes us realize that today's emphatic interest in memory does have consequences for the past. If the historical past once used to give coherence and legitimacy to family, community, nation, and state, in a discourse that Eric Hobsbawm called the "invention of tradition," then those formerly stable links have weakened today to the extent that national traditions and historical pasts are increasingly deprived of their geographic and political groundings, which are reorganized in the processes of cultural globalization. This may mean that these groundings are written over, erased, and forgotten, as the defenders of local heritage and national authenticity lament. Or it may mean that they are being renegotiated in the clash between globalizing forces and new productions and practices of local cultures. The form in which we think of the past is increasingly memory without borders rather than national history within borders. Modernity has brought with it a very real compression of time and space. But in the register of imaginaries, it has also expanded our horizons of time and space beyond the local, the national, and even the international. In certain ways, then, our contemporary obsessions with memory in the present may well be an indication that our ways of thinking and living temporality itself are undergoing a significant shift. This is what the whole academic debate about history vs. memory is subliminally all about, but one wouldn't know it by listening in. And yet, the most interesting aspect of the debate is what it may portend for the emergence of a new paradigm of thinking about time and space, history and geography in the twenty-first century.

Present Pasts and Our Modernity

This book is not interested in taking sides in the battle between historians and memorians. In my dual role as cultural historian and literary critic, I remain convinced that the explosion of memory discourses at the end of the twentieth century has added significantly to the ways we understand history and deal with the temporal dimensions of social and cultural life. Issues of memory have become part of public discourse and cultural life in ways rarely achieved by professional historiography alone. The title essay of this book explores that constellation in both its generative and its problematic dimensions.

At the same time, we need to acknowledge that the value of history is contested today in ways that differ from Nietzsche's critique of the archival and the monumental. The pressures on the traditional notion of history as objective and distinct from memory are so manifold today that it would be hard to weigh them all in their respective validity. The critique of historiography as a tool of domination and ideology, forcefully articulated by such socialist historians of the late nineteenth century as Walter Mehring in Germany, and later by Walter Benjamin in his radical, though overstated, political critique of all historicism; the post-Nietzschean attacks on linearity, on causality, and on the myths of origin or telos as articulated in the work of Foucault, Lyotard, and Derrida; the postcolonial critique of Western history as fundamentally implicated in an imperialist and racist Western modernity—these arguments are too well known to bear repeating here in detail. The attack on the history-modernity linkage has become such an *idée reçue* in certain intellectual circles today that one may well want to come to the defense of the embattled enterprise of writing history that, to my mind, remains an essential component of the power of memory discourse itself.

But something else still underlies the current political and conceptual arguments against historiography. The enlightened notion that one can learn from history has been so violently disproved both at the social and the political levels as well as in its experiential dimension that the very legitimacy of the historical enterprise is shaken. Who today can give a confident answer à la Friedrich Schiller to the question to what end one should study universal history? Although we would probably first want to question concepts like "universal" and "history" in line with one or the other of the above-mentioned critiques, we would no doubt continue and engage the past with gusto. Today's turn against history is very unlike Henry Ford's infamous "history is bunk." The desire for narratives of the past, for re-creations, re-readings, re-productions, seems boundless at every level of our culture. History in a certain canonical form may be delegitimized as far as its core pedagogical and philosophical mission is concerned, but the seduction of the archive and its trove of stories of human achievement and suffering has never been greater.

But what good is the memory archive? How can it deliver what history alone no longer seems to be able to offer? We know about the notorious unreliability of memory and the false promises of authenticity it is often endowed with. The issue today cannot be Nietzsche's creative forgetting, which would be nothing more than selective memory. Clearly, for Nietzsche the "free spirit" was the agent of creative forgetting, but such aristocratic intellectualism is both undesirable and unrealistic at a time when the threat of socially produced amnesia is just too great to ignore. Nor can the solution be a simple return to the promises of the future, as they are again being articulated today in the neoliberal discourse of economic and technological globalization. Such triumphalism of global flows is nothing but a form of uncreative forgetting that ignores the history of capitalist cycles and the crashes of technological utopias. Already the globalization fantasies of the 1990s have themselves become part of the memory archive and its cabinet of delusions. It is all the more important that at a time when an avalanche of memory discourses seems to have overwhelmed an earlier activist imagination of the future, we actually do remember the future and try to envision alternatives to the current status quo. It just will not do to replace the twentieth century's obsessions with the future with our newly found obsessions with the past. We need both past and future to articulate our political, social, and cultural dissatisfactions with the present state of the world. And while the hypertrophy of memory can lead to self-indulgence, melancholy fixations, and a problematic privileging of the traumatic dimension of life with no exit in sight, memory discourses are absolutely essential to imagine the future and to regain a strong temporal and spatial grounding of life and the imagination in a media and consumer society that increasingly voids temporality and collapses space.

Media of Cultural Memory

The essays of this book, which were written between 1996 and fall 2001 and which appear here in slightly modified or expanded form, attempt to counter such tendencies toward the voiding of time and the collapsing of spatial boundaries. They read specific urban phenomena, artworks, and literary texts that function as media of critical cultural memory today. The focus is exclusively on objects and practices in the present. One of the most interesting cultural phenomena of our day is the way in which memory and temporality have invaded spaces and media that seemed among the most stable and fixed: cities, monuments, architecture, and sculpture. After the waning of modernist fantasies about *creatio ex nihilo* and of the desire for the purity of new beginnings, we have come to read cities and buildings as palimpsests of space, monuments as transformable and transitory, and sculpture as subject to the vicissitudes of time. Of course, the majority of buildings are not palimpsests at all. As Freud once remarked, the same space cannot possibly have two different contents. But an urban imaginary in its temporal reach may well put different things in one place: memories of what there was before, imagined alternatives to what there is. The strong marks of present space merge in the imaginary with traces of the past, erasures, losses, and heterotopias. The center of Berlin and its reconstruction after unification provide a key example for the workings of such an imaginary.

Literary texts have never, not even in modernism, been able to deny their palimpsestic nature, and the philological problem of differing editions has always distinguished literature from buildings or monuments. The trope of the palimpsest is inherently literary and tied to writing, but it can also be fruitfully used to discuss configurations of urban spaces and their unfolding in time without making architecture and the city simply into text. Reading the city of Berlin or New York's Times Square as palimpsest does not mean to deny the essential materiality of extant buildings. Reading memory traces in the sculpture of Doris Salcedo or in the architectural landscaping project of Buenos Aires's Memory Park does not transform these objects into just another form of writing. My concern in all these essays is to respect the fundamental materiality and formal traditions of the different media of memory I discuss. My focus on reading palimpsests is not some imperialism of *écriture*, a reproach sometimes voiced against literary criticism after Derrida as well as against certain forms of deconstructive architecture. It is rather the conviction that literary techniques of reading historically, intertextually, constructively, and deconstructively at the same time can be woven into our understanding of urban spaces as lived spaces that shape collective imaginaries. In a more pragmatic vein, the urban essays in this book attempt to understand the fundamental temporality of even those human endeavors that pretend to transcend time through their material reality and relative durability.

One other thing remains to be said as I look back on more than a decade of critical work on memory. My overall choice of topics and memory media in this book is guided by the conviction that too much of the contemporary memory discourse focuses on the personal—on testimony, memoir, subjectivity, traumatic memory—either in poststructuralist psychoanalytic perspective or in attempts to shore up a therapeutic popular sense of the authentic and experiential. If the 1980s were the decade of a happy postmodern pluralism, the 1990s seemed to be haunted by trauma as the dark underside of neoliberal triumphalism. The concern with trauma radiated out from a multinational, ever more ubiquitous Holocaust discourse. It was energized, in the United States as in Latin America or South Africa after apartheid, by the intense interest in witness and survivor testimonies, and it merged with the discourses about AIDS, slavery, family violence, child abuse, recovered memory syndrome, and so on. The privileging of trauma formed a thick discursive network with those other master-signifiers of the 1990s, the abject and the uncanny, all of which have to do with repression, specters, and a present repetitively haunted by the past.

Surely, the prevalence of the concern with trauma must be due to the fact that trauma as a psychic phenomenon is located on the threshold between remembering and forgetting, seeing and not seeing, transparency and occlusion, experience and its absence in repetition. But trauma cannot be the central category in addressing the larger memory discourse. It has been all too tempting to some to think of trauma as the hidden core of all memory. After all, both memory and trauma are predicated on the absence of that which is negotiated in memory or in the traumatic symptom. Both are marked by instability, transitoriness, and structures of repetition. But to collapse memory into trauma, I think, would unduly confine our understanding of memory, marking it too exclusively in terms of pain, suffering, and loss. It would deny human agency and lock us into compulsive repetition. Memory, whether individual or generational, political or public, is always more than only the prison house of the past.

The more serious political question emerges when the psychoanalytic notion of trauma is simply transferred to the historical arena. We are used to distinguishing between personal memory and public memory. But what happens when we talk about historical trauma? What is at stake when we consider, as we seem to do ever more frequently, the whole history of the twentieth century under the sign of trauma, with the Holocaust increasingly functioning as the ultimate cipher of traumatic unspeakability or unrepresentability? And what if this assessment is then extended—under the guise of various forms of apocalyptic and anarchic thinking—to the whole history of enlightenment modernity: modernity as the trauma that victimizes the world, that we cannot leave behind, that causes all of our symptoms? The newly found popularity of Horkheimer and Adorno's *Dialectic of Enlightenment*, the cult status of Benjamin's angel of history, and the trauma work of Cathy Caruth, Shoshana Felman, and others all raise the suspicion that we are simply rearticulating Freudian phylogenetic fantasies in a different, significantly darker key. Ultimately, this is philosophy of history entering through the back door—not via Hegel or Marx, to be sure, but via Freud. This approach to history as trauma, I would suggest, does not help much to understand the political layers of memory discourse in our time, although it may well represent one of its major articulations.

At the same time, explorations of memory in our world cannot do without the notion of historical trauma. The focus on trauma is legitimate where nations or groups of people are trying to come to terms with a history of violence suffered or violence perpetrated. But the transnational discourse of human rights may give us a better handle on such matters than the transfer of psychoanalysis into the world of politics and history. For it is precisely the function of public memory discourses to allow individuals to break out of traumatic repetitions. Human rights activism, truth commissions, and juridical proceedings are better methods for dealing with historical trauma. Another is the creation of objects, artworks, memorials, public spaces of commemoration, as they are discussed in this book. Here the analysis of how memory and forgetting pervade real public space, the world of objects, and the urban world we live in becomes crucial. The reconstruction of Berlin as the German capital after unification provides a perhaps unique case in which this latter dimension has produced a paradigmatic public memory space, even if many of the architectural and planning results have left us more than dissatisfied.

Perhaps for that reason, I could not bring myself to exclude more properly literary readings from this book. Actually, the literary essays on Spiegelman and Sebald should serve to highlight the difference that pertains between reading texts and reading urban space. They also show how contemporary texts that mix language and image foreground the palimpsestic nature of all writing to great effect and in creatively new ways. Both are memory texts in the most emphatic sense, working in complex ways on the issue of history and its representation—the history of the Holocaust in the case of Spiegelman and the history of the saturation bombings of German cities in World War II in the case of Sebald. Both authors are fundamentally concerned with haunted space and spatial imaginaries. Both texts acknowledge that, contrary to the belief of many historians, representations of the visible will always show residues and traces of the invisible. Spiegelman's and Sebald's texts haunt us because they themselves are haunted. A literature that is both post-mimetic and postmodernist, both historical and attuned to the erasures of the historical record, partakes in the force play of remembrance and forgetting, vision and blindness, transparency and opaqueness of the world.

At the same time, we cannot be entirely confident that contemporary memory discourses and the cultural products they generate will fare better than traditional history in shaping public debate in the long run. The paradox is that memory discourses themselves partake in the detemporalizing processes that characterize a culture of consumption and obsolescence. Memory as re-presentation, as making present, is always in danger of collapsing the constitutive tension between past and present, especially when the imagined past is sucked into the timeless present of the all-pervasive virtual space of consumer culture. Thus we need to discriminate among memory practices in order to strengthen those that counteract the tendencies in our culture to foster uncreative forgetting, the bliss of amnesia, and what the German philosopher Peter Sloterdijk once called "enlightened false consciousness." I hope that in some small measure this book may contribute to such discrimination. For who wants to end up in the land of the lotus-eaters enjoying one's own oblivion before the real journey into the past has even begun, that journey into the past without which there can be no imagining the future?

Present Pasts: Media, Politics, Amnesia

I

One of the most surprising cultural and political phenomena of recent years has been the emergence of memory as a key cultural and political concern in Western societies, a turning toward the past that stands in stark contrast to the privileging of the future so characteristic of earlier decades of twentieth-century modernity. From the early twentieth century's apocalyptic myths of radical breakthrough and the emergence of the "new man" in Europe via the murderous phantasms of racial or class purification in National Socialism and Stalinism to the post–World War II American paradigm of modernization, modernist culture was energized by what one might call "present futures."[1] Since the 1980s, it seems, the focus has shifted from present futures to present pasts, and this shift in the experience and sensibility of time needs to be explained historically and phenomenologically.[2]

But the contemporary focus on memory and temporality is mostly absent from much recent innovative work on categories of space, maps, geographies, borders, trade routes, migrations, displacements, and diasporas in the context of postcolonial and cultural studies. Not so long ago in the United States, there was a widespread consensus that in order to understand postmodern culture, the focus had to be shifted from the problematics of time and memory ascribed to an earlier form of high modernism to that of space as key to the postmodern moment.[3] But as the work of geographers such as David Harvey has shown,[4] we would separate time and space at great peril to a full understanding of either modern or postmodern culture. As fundamentally contingent categories of historically rooted perception, time and space are always bound up with each other in complex ways, and the intensity of border-crossing memory discourses that characterize so much of contemporary culture in so many different parts of the world today proves the point. Indeed, issues of differing temporalities and alternatively paced modernities have emerged as key to a new rigorous understanding of the long-term processes of globalization that tries to be more than just an update of Western modernization paradigms.[5]

Memory discourses of a new kind first emerged in the West after the 1960s in the wake of decolonization and the new social movements and their search for alternative and revisionist histories. The search for other traditions and the tradition of "others" was accompanied by multiple statements about endings: the end of history, the death of the subject, the end of the work of art, the end of metanarratives.[6] Such claims were frequently understood all too literally, but in their polemical thrust and replication of the ethos of avant-gardism, they pointed directly to the ongoing recodification of the past after modernism.

Memory discourses accelerated in Europe and the United States by the early 1980s, energized then primarily by the ever-broadening debate about the Holocaust (triggered by the TV series *Holocaust* and, somewhat later, by the testimony movement), as well as by a whole series of politically loaded and widely covered fortieth and fiftieth anniversaries relating to the history of the Third Reich: Hitler's rise to power in 1933 and the Nazis' infamous book burnings, remembered in 1983; Kristallnacht, the organized pogrom of 1938 against Germany's Jews, publicly commemorated in 1988; the Wannsee Conference of 1942, which had initiated the Final Solution, remembered in 1992 with the opening of a museum in the Wannsee villa where the conference had taken place; the Allied invasion of Normandy in 1944, remembered with grand spectacle by the Allies, but without any Russian presence, in 1994; the end of World War II in 1945, remembered in 1985 with a stirring speech by the German president and again in 1995 with a whole series of international events in Europe and Japan. Such mostly "German anniversaries," the historians' debate of 1986, the fall of the Berlin Wall in 1989, and German national reunification in

1990,[7] received intense coverage in the international media, stirring up post–World War II codifications of national history in France, Austria, Italy, Japan, even the United States, and most recently Switzerland. The Holocaust Memorial Museum in Washington, D.C., planned during the 1980s and inaugurated in 1993, gave rise to the debate about the Americanization of the Holocaust.[8] But the resonances of Holocaust memory did not stop there. At this point one must indeed raise the question to what extent one can now speak of a globalization of Holocaust discourse.

The recurrence of genocidal politics in Rwanda, Bosnia, and Kosovo in the allegedly posthistorical 1990s has kept the Holocaust memory discourse alive, contaminating it and extending it past its original reference point. It is interesting to note how in the case of the organized massacres in Rwanda and Bosnia in the early 1990s, comparisons with the Holocaust were at first fiercely resisted by politicians, the media, and much of the public, not because of the undeniable historical differences, but rather because of a desire to resist intervention.[9] NATO's "humanitarian" intervention in Kosovo and its legitimation, on the other hand, have been largely dependent on Holocaust memory. Streams of refugees across borders, women and children packed into trains for deportation, stories of atrocities, systematic rape, and wanton destruction all mobilized a politics of guilt in Europe and the United States associated with nonintervention in the 1930s and 1940s and the failure to intervene in the Bosnian war of 1992. The Kosovo war thus confirms the increasing power of memory culture in the late 1990s, but it also raises thorny issues about using the Holocaust as a universal trope for historical trauma.

The globalization of memory works as well in two other related senses that illustrate what I would call the globalization paradox. On the one hand, the Holocaust has become a cipher for the twentieth century as a whole and for the failure of the project of enlightenment. It serves as proof of Western civilization's failure to practice anamnesis, to reflect on its constitutive inability to live in peace with difference and otherness, and to draw the consequences from the insidious relationship among enlightened modernity, racial oppression, and organized violence.[10] On the other hand, this totalizing dimension of Holocaust discourse so prevalent in much postmodern thought is accompanied by a dimension that particularizes and localizes. It is precisely the emergence of the Holocaust as a universal trope that allows Holocaust memory to latch on to specific local situations that are historically distant and politically distinct from the original event. In the transnational movement of memory discourses, the Holocaust loses its quality as index of the specific historical event and begins to function as metaphor for other traumatic histories and memories. The Holocaust as a universal trope is a prerequisite for its decentering and its use as a powerful prism through which we may look at other instances of genocide. The global and the local aspects of Holocaust memory have entered into new constellations that beg to be analyzed case by case. While the comparison with the Holocaust may rhetorically energize some discourses of traumatic memory, it may also serve as a screen memory or simply block insight into specific local histories.

When it comes to present pasts, memory of the Holocaust and its place in the reassessment of Western modernity, however, is not the whole story. Many subplots make up the current memory narrative in its broadest scope and distinguish our times quite clearly from earlier decades of this century. Let me just list a few of the salient phenomena. Since the 1970s in Europe and the United States we have the historicizing restoration of old urban centers, whole museum villages and landscapes, various national heritage and patrimony enterprises, the wave of new museum architecture that shows no signs of receding, the boom in retro fashions and repro furniture, the mass-marketing of nostalgia, the obsessive self-musealization per video recorder, memoir writing, and confessional literature, the rise of autobiography and of the postmodern historical novel with its uneasy negotiation between fact and fiction, the spread of memory practices in the visual arts often centered on the medium of photography, and the increase of historical documentaries on television, including (in the United States) a channel dedicated entirely to history, the History Channel. On the traumatic side of memory culture and beside the ever more ubiquitous Holocaust discourse we have the vast psychoanalytic literature on trauma; the controversy about recovered memory syndrome; the historical and current work related to genocide, AIDs, slavery, and sexual abuse; the ever more numerous public controversies about politically painful anniversaries, commemorations, and memorials; the latest plethora of apologies for the past by church leaders and politicians in France, Japan, and the United States. And, finally, bringing together memory entertainment and trauma, we have had the worldwide obsession with the sinking of a presumably unsinkable steamship that marked the end of another gilded age. One cannot be quite sure whether the international success of the film *Titanic* is a metaphor for memories of modernity gone awry or whether it articulates the metropolis's own anxieties about the future displaced to the past. No doubt, the world is being musealized, and we all play our parts in it. Total recall seems to be the goal. So is this an archivist's fantasy gone mad? Or is there perhaps something else at stake in this desire to pull all these various pasts into the present? Something that is specific to the structuring of memory and temporality today and that has not been experienced in the same way in past ages?

Frequently such obsessions with memory and the past are explained as a function of the latest fin de siècle, but I think one has to probe deeper to come to terms with what I will call the "culture of memory" that has become so pervasive in North Atlantic societies since the late 1970s. What here appears largely as an increasingly successful marketing of memory by the Western culture industry in the context of what German cultural sociology has called our *Erlebnisgesellschaft* acquires a more explicitly political inflection in other parts of the world.[11] Especially since 1989, the issues of memory and forgetting have emerged as dominant concerns in postcommunist countries in Eastern Europe and the former Soviet Union; they remain key politically in the Middle East; they dominate public discourse in post-apartheid South Africa with its Truth and Reconciliation Commission, and they are all-present in Rwanda and Nigeria; they energize the race debate that has erupted in Australia around the issue of the "stolen generation"; they burden the relationship among Japan and China and Korea, and they determine, to varying degrees, the cultural and political debate about the "desaparecidos" and their children in "post-dictatura" societies in Latin America, raising fundamental questions about human rights violations, justice, and collective responsibility.

The geographic spread of the culture of memory is as wide as memory's political uses are varied, ranging from a mobilization of mythic pasts to support aggressively chauvinist or fundamentalist politics (e.g., postcommunist Serbia, Hindu populism in India) to fledgling attempts, in Argentina and Chile, to create public spheres of "real" memory that will counter the politics of forgetting, pursued by postdictatorship regimes either through "reconciliation" and official amnesties or through repressive silencing.[12] But the fault line between mythic past and real past is not always easy to draw—which is one of the conundrums of any politics of memory anywhere. The real can be mythologized, just as the mythic may engender strong reality effects. In sum, memory has become a cultural obsession of monumental proportions across the globe.

At the same time it is important to recognize that although memory discourses appear to be global in one register, at their core they remain tied to the histories of specific nations and states. As particular nations struggle to create democratic polities in the wake of histories of mass extermination, apartheid, military dictatorship, or totalitarianism, they are faced, as Germany has been and still is since World War II, with the unprecedented task of securing the legitimacy and future of their emergent polity by finding ways to commemorate and adjudicate past wrongs. Whatever the differences may be between postwar Germany and South Africa, Argentina or Chile, the *political* site of memory practices is still national, not postnational or global. This does have implications for interpretive work. Although the Holocaust as a universal trope of traumatic history has migrated into other, nonrelated contexts, one must always ask whether and how the trope enhances or hinders local memory practices and struggles, or whether and how it may help and hinder at the same time. National memory debates are always shot through with the effects of the global media and their focus on themes such as genocide and ethnic cleansing, migration and minority rights, victimization and accountability. However different and site-specific the causes may be, this does suggest that globalization and the strong reassessment of the respective national, regional, or local past will have to be thought together. This in turn raises the question whether contemporary memory cultures in general can be read as reaction formations to economic globalization. Such is the terrain on which new comparative work on the mechanisms and tropes of historical trauma and national memory practices could be pursued.

II

If the time-consciousness of high modernity in the West tried to secure the future, then one could argue that the time-consciousness of the late twentieth century involves the no less perilous task of taking responsibility for the past. Both attempts inevitably are haunted by failure. Thus a second point must be made immediately. The turn toward memory and the past comes with a great paradox. Ever more frequently, critics accuse this very contemporary memory culture of amnesia, anesthesia, or numbing. They chide its inability and unwillingness to remember, and they lament the loss of historical consciousness. The amnesia reproach is invariably couched in a critique of the media, while it is precisely these media—from print and television to CD-ROMs and the Internet—that make ever more memory available to us day by day. But what if both observations were true, if the boom in memory were inevitably accompanied by a boom in forgetting? What if the relationship between memory and forgetting were actually being transformed under cultural pressures in which new information technologies, media politics, and fast-paced consumption are beginning to take their toll? After all, many of the mass-marketed memories we consume are "imagined memories" to begin with, and thus more easily forgettable than lived memories.[13] But then Freud already taught us that memory and forgetting are indissolubly linked to each other, that memory is but another form of forgetting, and forgetting a form of hidden memory. Yet what Freud described universally as the psychic processes of remembering, repression, and forgetting in individuals is writ large in contemporary consumer societies as a public phenomenon of unprecedented proportions that begs to be read historically.

Wherever one looks, the contemporary public obsession with memory clashes with an intense public panic of oblivion, and one may well wonder which came first. Is it the fear of forgetting that triggers the desire to remember, or is it perhaps the other way around? Could it be that the surfeit of memory in this media-saturated culture creates such overload that the memory system itself is in constant danger of imploding, thus triggering fear of forgetting? Whatever the answer to such questions, it seems clear that older sociological approaches to collective memory—approaches (such as Maurice Halbwachs's) that posit relatively stable formations of social and group memories—are not adequate to grasp the current dynamic of media and temporality, memory, lived time, and forgetting. The clashing and ever more fragmented memory politics of specific social and ethnic groups raises the question whether forms of collective consensual memory are even still possible today, and, if not, whether and in what form social and cultural cohesion can be guaranteed without them. Media memory alone clearly will not suffice, even though the media occupy ever larger chunks of the social and political perception of the world.

The very structures of public media memory make it quite understandable that our secular culture today, obsessed with memory as it is, is also somehow in the grips of a fear, even a terror, of forgetting. This fear of forgetting articulates itself paradigmatically around issues of the Holocaust in Europe and the United States or the *desaparecidos* in Latin America. Both share the absence of a proper burial site, so key to the nurturing of human memory, a fact that may help explain the strong presence of the Holocaust in Argentinean debates. But the fear of oblivion and disappearance operates in a different register as well. For the more we are asked to remember in the wake of the information explosion and the marketing of memory, the more we seem to be in danger of forgetting and the stronger the need to forget. At issue is the distinction between usable pasts and disposable data. My hypothesis here is that we are trying to counteract this fear and danger of forgetting with survival strategies of public and private memorialization. The turn toward memory is subliminally energized by the desire to anchor ourselves in a world characterized by an increasing instability of time and the fracturing of lived space. At the same time, we know that such strategies of memorialization may in the end themselves be transitory and incomplete. So I must come back to the question: why? And especially: why now? Why this obsession with memory and the past and why this fear of forgetting? Why are we building museums as if there were no tomorrow? And why is it that the Holocaust has only now become something like a ubiquitous cipher for our memories of the twentieth century, in ways unimaginable even twenty years ago?

III

Whatever the social and political causes of the memory boom in its various subplots, geographies, and sectorings may have been, one thing is certain: we cannot discuss personal, generational, or public memory separately from the enormous influence of the new media as carriers of all forms of memory. Thus it is no longer possible for instance to think of the Holocaust or of any other historical trauma as a serious ethical and political issue apart from the multiple ways it is now linked to commodification and spectacularization in films, museums, docudramas, Internet sites, photography books, comics, fiction, even fairy tales (Roberto Benigni's *La vita è bella*) and pop songs. But even if the Holocaust has been endlessly commodified, this does not mean that each and every commodification inevitably banalizes it as an historical event. There is no pure space outside of commodity culture, however much we may desire such a space. Much depends therefore on the specific strategies of representation and commodification pursued and on the context in which they are staged. Similarly, the presumably trivial *Erlebnisgesellschaft* of mass-marketed lifestyles, spectacles, and fleeting events is not devoid of a substantive lived reality that underlies its surface manifestations. My argument here is this: the problem is not solved by simply opposing serious memory to trivial memory, the way historians sometime oppose history to memory *tout court*, to memory understood as the subjective and trivial stuff out of which the historian makes the real thing. We cannot simply pit the serious Holocaust museum against Disneyfied theme parks. For this would only reproduce the old high/low dichotomy of modernist culture in a new guise, as it did in the heated debate that pitted Claude Lanzmann's *Shoah* as a proper representation (because a nonrepresentation) of Holocaust memory against Steven Spielberg's *Schindler's List* as its commercial trivialization. Once we acknowledge the constitutive gap between reality and its representation in language or image, we must in principle be open to many different possibilities of representing the real and its memories. This is not to say that anything goes. The question of quality remains one to be decided case by case. But the semiotic gap cannot be closed by any orthodoxy of correct representation. To argue as much amounts to Holocaust modernism.[14] Indeed, phenomena such as *Schindler's List* and Spielberg's visual archive of Holocaust survivor testimonies compel us to think of traumatic memory and entertainment memory together as occupying the same public space, rather than to see them as mutually exclusive phenomena. Key questions of contemporary culture are located precisely at the threshold between traumatic memory and the commercial media. It is too easy to argue that the fun events and spectacles of contemporary media societies exist only to provide relief to a social and political body haunted by deep memories of violence and genocide perpetrated in its name, or that they are mounted only to repress such memories. For trauma is marketed as much as the fun is, and not even for different memory consumers. It is also too easy to suggest that the specters of the past now haunting modern societies in heretofore unknown force actually articulate, by way of displacement, a growing fear of the future at a time when the belief in modernity's progress is deeply shaken.

We do know that the media do not transport public memory innocently. They shape it in their very structure and form. And here—in line with McLuhan's well-worn point that the medium is the message—it becomes highly significant that the power of our most advanced electronics depends entirely on quantities of memory. Bill Gates may just be the latest incarnation of the old American ideal—more is better. But "more" is now measured in memory bytes and in the power to recycle the past. Gates's much-advertised purchase of the largest collection of original photographs ever is a case in point: in the move from the photograph to its digital recycling, Walter Benjamin's art of mechanical reproduction (photography) has regained an aura of originality. Which goes to show that Benjamin's famous argument about the loss or decay of the aura in modernity was always only half the story; it forgot that modernization itself created the auratic effect to begin with. Today, digitalization makes the "original" photograph auratic. After all, as Benjamin also knew, the culture industry of Weimar Germany already then needed the auratic as a marketing strategy.

So let me indulge here for a moment in the old culture industry argument that Adorno mounted against what he thought to be Benjamin's unwarranted optimism about technological media. If today the idea of the total archive makes the triumphalists of cyberspace embrace global fantasies à la McLuhan, the profit interests of memory's mass marketeers seem to be more pertinent in explaining the success of the memory syndrome. Simply put, the past is selling better than the future. But for how long, one wonders.

Take the headline of a spoof posted on the Internet: "U.S. Department of Retro Warns: We May Be Running Out of a Past." The first paragraph reads: "At a press conference Monday, U.S. Retro Secretary Anson Williams issued a strongly worded warning of an imminent 'National retro crisis,' cautioning that 'if current levels of U.S. retro consumption are allowed to continue unchecked, we may run entirely out of past by as soon as 2005'." Not to worry. We already have the marketing of pasts that never existed: Witness the recent introduction of the Aerobleu product line, 1940s and 1950s nostalgia cleverly organized around a fictional Paris jazz club that never existed, but where all the jazz greats of the bebop age are said to have performed: a product line replete with original diaries, original cuts on CDs, and original memorabilia, all available in the United States at any local Barnes and Noble.[15] "Original remakes" are in, and not only as merchandise: as cultural theorists and critics we are obsessed with re-presentation, repetition, replication, and the culture of the copy, with or without original.

With all this going on, it seems fair to ask: once the memory boom is history, as no doubt it will be, will anyone have remembered anything at all? If all of the past can be made over, aren't we just creating our own illusions of the past while getting stuck in an ever-shrinking present—the present of short-term recycling for profit, the present of in-time production, instant entertainment, and placebos for our sense of dread and insecurity that lies barely underneath the surface of this new gilded age at another fin de siècle? Computers, we were told, would not know the difference between the year 2000 and the year 1900—but do we?

IV

The critics of late capitalist amnesia doubt that Western media culture has anything left resembling "real" memory or a strong sense of history. Drawing on the standard Adornean argument that commodification equals forgetting, they argue that the marketing of memory generates nothing but amnesia. I do not find this argument convincing. It leaves too much out. It is too easy to blame the dilemma we find ourselves in on the machinations of the culture industry and the proliferation of the new media. Something else must be at stake that produces the desire for the past in the first place and that makes us respond so favorably to the memory markets. That something, I would suggest, is a slow but palpable transformation of temporality in our lives, brought on by the complex intersections of technological change, mass media, and new patterns of consumption, work, and global mobility. There may indeed be good reasons to think that the drive to memorialize has a more beneficial and generative dimension as well. However much our current concerns with memory may involve a displaced fear of the future, and however dubious the proposition may now strike us that we can learn from history, memory culture fulfills an important function in the current transformation of temporal experience that has followed in the wake of the new media's impact on human perception and sensibility.

In the following, then, I would like to suggest some ways to think about the relationship between our privileging of memory and the past on the one hand and the potential impact of the new media on perception and temporality on the other. It is a complex story. Applying the blistering Adornean critique of the culture industry to what one could now call the memory industry would be as one-sided and unsatisfactory as relying on Benjamin's trust in the emancipatory potential of the new media. Adorno's critique is right as far as the mass-marketing of cultural products is concerned, but it does not help explain the rise of the memory syndrome within the culture industry. His theoretical emphasis on Marxist categories of exchange value and reification actually blocks issues of temporality and memory, and he does not pay enough attention to the specifics of media and their relation to the structures of perception and everyday life in consumer societies. Benjamin, on the other hand, is right in attributing a cognitively enabling dimension to memory, retro, and what in the "Theses on the Philosophy of History" he calls the tiger's leap into the past, but he wants to achieve it through the very media of reproducibility that, to him, represent the futurist promise and enable socialist political mobilization. Rather than siding with Benjamin against Adorno or vice versa, as so often happens, I would make the tension between their arguments productive for an analysis of the present.

Here I will turn to an argument first articulated by conservative German philosopher Hermann Lübbe in the early 1980s. Already then, as others were debating the future promises of postmodernism, Lübbe described what he called "musealization" as central to the shifting temporal sensibility of our time.[16] He showed how musealization was no longer bound to the institution of the museum, understood in the narrow sense, but had come to infiltrate all areas of everyday life. Lübbe's diagnosis posited an expansive historicism of our contemporary culture, and he claimed that never before had a cultural present been obsessed with the past to a similar extent. Lübbe argued that modernization is inevitably accompanied by the atrophy of valid traditions, a loss of rationality, and the entropy of stable and lasting life experiences. The ever-increasing speed of technical, scientific, and cultural innovation produces ever larger quantities of the soon-to-be-obsolete, and it objectively shrinks the chronological expansion of what can be considered the (cutting-edge) present at any given time.

On the surface, this argument seems quite plausible. It reminds me of an incident a few years ago when I went to buy a computer in an electronics store in New York. The purchase proved to be more difficult than I had anticipated. Whatever was on display was relentlessly described by the sales personnel as already obsolete, i.e., museal, by comparison with the imminently expected and so much more powerful next product line. This seemed to give new meaning to the old ethic of postponing gratification. I was not persuaded, and made my purchase, a two-year-old model that had everything I needed and more and whose price had recently been cut in half. I bought "obsolete," and thus I was not surprised recently to see my 1995 butterfly IBM Thinkpad exhibited in the design section of the Museum of Modern Art in New York. The shelf life of consumer objects has been radically shortened, and with it the extension of the present, in Lübbe's sense, has shrunk at the same time that computer memory and public memory discourses keep expanding.

What Lübbe described as musealization can now be easily mapped onto the phenomenal rise of the memory discourse within the discipline of historiography itself. Historical memory research is international in scope. My hypothesis is that, in this prominence of academic mnemohistory as well, memory and musealization together are called upon to provide a bulwark against obsolescence and disappearance, to counter our deep anxiety about the speed of change and the ever-shrinking horizons of time and space.

Lübbe's argument about the shrinking extension of the present points to a great paradox: the more the present of advanced consumer capitalism prevails over the past and the future, sucking both into an expanding synchronous space, the weaker its grip on itself, the less stability or identity it provides for contemporary subjects. The German filmmaker and writer Alexander Kluge has spoken of the attack of the present on the rest of time. There is both too much and too little present at the same time, a historically novel situation that creates unbearable tensions in our "structure of feeling," as Raymond Williams would call it. In Lübbe's theory, the museum compensates for this loss of stability by offering traditional forms of cultural identity to a destabilized modern subject. Yet Lübbe fails to acknowledge that these cultural traditions have themselves been affected by modernization through digital and commodified recycling. His idea of musealization and French historian Pierre Nora's notion of *lieux de mémoire* actually share the compensatory sensibility that acknowledges a loss of national or communal identity, but trusts in our ability to make up for it. Nora's *lieux de mémoire* compensate for the loss of *milieux de mémoire,* just as Lübbe's musealization compensates for the loss of lived tradition.

This conservative argument about shifts in temporal sensibility needs to be taken out of its binary framing (*lieux* vs. *milieux* in Nora, entropy of the past vs. compensatory musealization in Lübbe) and pushed in a different direction, one that does not rely on a discourse of loss and that accepts the fundamental shift in structures of feeling, experience, and perception as they characterize our simultaneously expanding and shrinking present. The conservative belief that cultural musealization can provide compensation for the ravages of accelerating modernization in the social world is just too simple and too ideological. It fails to recognize that any secure sense of the past itself is being destabilized by our musealizing culture industry and by the media that function as leading players in the morality play of memory. Musealization itself is sucked into the vortex of an ever-accelerating circulation of images, spectacles, events, and is thus always in danger of losing its ability to guarantee cultural stability over time.

V

It bears repeating that at the end of the millennium, the coordinates of space and time structuring our lives are increasingly subjected to new kinds of pressures. Space and time are fundamental categories of human experience and perception, but far from being immutable, they are very much subject to historical change. One of modernity's permanent laments concerns the loss of a better past, the memory of living in a securely circumscribed place, with a sense of stable boundaries and a place-bound culture with its regular flow of time and a core of permanent relations. Perhaps such days have always been dream rather than reality, a phantasmagoria of loss generated by modernity itself rather than by its prehistory. But the dream does have staying power, and what I have called the culture of memory may well be, at least in part, its contemporary incarnation. The issue, however, is not the loss of some golden age of stability and permanence. The issue is rather the attempt, as we face the very real processes of time-space compression, to secure some continuity within time, to provide some extension of lived space within which we can breathe and move.

For surely enough, the end of the twentieth century does not give us easy access to the trope of a golden age. Memories of the twentieth century confront us not with a better life, but with a unique history of genocide and mass destruction that mars a priori any attempt to glorify the past. After the experiences of World War I and the Great Depression, of Stalinism, Nazism, and genocide on an unprecedented scale, after the trials of decolonization and the histories of atrocities and repression they have brought to our consciousness, the view of Western modernity and its promises has darkened considerably within the West itself. Even the current gilded age in the United States cannot quite shake the memories of the tremors that have rattled the myth of permanent progress since the late 1960s and 1970s. Witnessing the ever-widening gap between rich and poor, the barely controlled meltdown of whole regional and national economies, and the return of war to the continent that spawned two world wars in the last century has surely brought with it a significant entropy of our sense of future possibilities.

In an era of ethnic cleansings and refugee crises, mass migrations and global mobility for ever more people, the experience of displacement and relocation, migration and diaspora seems no longer the exception but the rule. But such phenomena do not tell the whole story. As spatial barriers weaken and space itself is gobbled up by time ever more compressed, a new kind of malaise is taking root in the heart of the metropolis. The discontents of metropolitan civilization at the end of the century no longer seem to stem primarily from pervasive feelings of guilt and super-ego repression, as Freud had it in his analysis of classical Western modernity and its dominant mode of subject formation. Franz Kafka and Woody Allen belong to an earlier age. Our own discontents flow instead from informational and perceptual overload combined with a cultural acceleration that neither our psyche nor our senses are adequately equipped to handle. The faster we are pushed into a global future that does not inspire confidence, the stronger we feel the desire to slow down, the more we turn to memory for comfort. But what comfort is to be had from memories of the twentieth century?! And what are the alternatives? How are we to negotiate the rapid change and turnover in what Georg Simmel called objective culture while at the same time satisfying what I take to be the fundamental need of modern societies to live in extended forms of temporality and to secure a space, however permeable, from which to speak and to act? There is no one simple answer to such a question, but memory—individual, generational, public, cultural, and, still inevitably, national memory—must surely be part of it. Perhaps one day there will even emerge something like a global memory as the different parts of the world are drawn ever tighter together. But any such global memory will always be prismatic and heterogeneous rather than holistic or universal.

In the meantime we have to ask: how should even local, regional, or national memories be secured, structured, and represented? Of course, this is a fundamentally political question about the nature of the public sphere, about democracy and its future, about the changing shape of nationhood, citizenship, and identity. The answers will depend to a large degree on local constellations, but the global spread of memory discourses indicates that something more is at stake.

Some have turned to the idea of the archive as counterweight to the ever-increasing pace of change, as a site of temporal and spatial preservation. From the point of view of the archive, forgetting is the ultimate transgression. But how reliable or foolproof are our digitalized archives? Computers are barely fifty years old and already we need "data archaeologists" to unlock the mysteries of early programming: just think of the notorious Y2K problem that recently haunted our computerized bureaucracies. Billions of dollars were spent to prevent computer networks from going into retro mode, from mistaking the year 2000 for 1900. Or consider the almost insuperable difficulties German authorities now have decoding the vast body of electronic records from the former East German state, a world that disappeared together with its Soviet-built mainframe computers and its East German office systems. Reflecting on such phenomena, a senior manager charged with information technology at the Canadian archives was recently quoted as saying: "It's one of the great ironies of the information age. If we don't find methods for enduring preservation of electronic records, this may be the era without a memory."[17] The threat of oblivion thus emerges from the very technology to which we entrust the vast body of contemporary records and data, that most significant part of the cultural memory of our time.

The current transformations of the temporal imaginary brought on by virtual space and time may highlight the enabling dimension of memory culture. Whatever their specific occasion, cause, or context, the intense memory practices we witness in so many different parts of the world today articulate a fundamental crisis of an earlier structure of temporality that marked the age of high modernity with its trust in progress and development, with its celebration of the new as utopian, as radically and irreducibly other, and with its unshaken belief in some telos of history. Politically, many memory practices today counteract the triumphalism of modernization theory in its latest guise of the discourse of "globalization." Culturally, they express the growing need for spatial and temporal anchoring in a world of increasing flux in ever denser networks of compressed time and space. As historiography has shed an earlier reliance on teleological master-narratives and has grown more skeptical of nationalist framings of its subject matter, today's critical memory cultures, with their emphases on human rights, on minority and gender issues, and on reassessing various national and international pasts go a long way to provide a welcome impetus for writing history in a new key and thus for guaranteeing a future of memory. In the best-case scenario, the cultures of memory are intimately linked, in many parts of the world, to processes of democratization and struggles for human rights, to expanding and strengthening the public spheres of civil society. Slowing down rather than speeding up, expanding the nature of public debate, trying to heal the wounds inflicted in the past, nurturing and expanding livable space rather than destroy it for the sake of some future promise, securing "quality time"—those seem to be unmet cultural needs in a globalizing world, and local memories are intimately linked to their articulation.

But the past cannot give us what the future has failed to deliver. There is no avoiding coming back to the downside of what some would call a memory epidemic, and this brings me back to Nietzsche, whose second untimely meditation on the use and abuse of history, often quoted in contemporary memory debates, may be as untimely as ever. Clearly, the memory fever of Western media societies is not a consuming historical fever in Nietzsche's sense, which could be cured by productive forgetting. It is rather a mnemonic fever caused by the cyber-virus of amnesia that at times threatens to consume memory itself. Therefore we now need productive remembering more than productive forgetting. In retrospect we can see how the historical fever of Nietzsche's times functioned to invent national traditions in Europe, to legitimize the imperial nation-states, and to give cultural coherence to conflictive societies in the throes of the Industrial Revolution and colonial expansion. By comparison, the mnemonic convulsions of North

Atlantic culture today seem mostly chaotic, fragmentary, and free-floating across our screens. Even in places where memory practices have a very clear political focus such as South Africa, Argentina, Chile, and most recently Guatemala, they are affected, and to a degree even created by, international media coverage and its memory obsessions. As I suggested earlier, securing the past is no less risky an enterprise than securing the future. Memory, after all, can be no substitute for justice, and justice itself will inevitably be entangled in the unreliability of memory. But even where cultural memory practices lack an explicit political focus, they do express a society's need for temporal anchoring when in the wake of the information revolution and an ever-increasing time-space compression, the relationship among past, present, and future is being transformed beyond recognition.

In that sense, local and national memory practices contest the myths of cyber-capitalism and globalization and their denial of time, space, and place. No doubt, some new configuration of time and space will eventually emerge from this negotiation. New technologies of transportation and communication have always transformed the human perception of time and space in modernity. This was as true for the railroad and the telephone, the radio and the airplane as it will be true for cyberspace and cyber-time. New technologies and new media are also always met by anxieties and fear that later prove to have been unwarranted or even ridiculous. Our age will be no exception.

At the same time, cyberspace alone is not the appropriate model for imagining the global future. Its notion of memory is misleading, a false promise. Lived memory is active, alive, embodied in the social—that is, in individuals, families, groups, nations, and regions. These are the memories needed to construct differential local futures in a global world. There is no doubt that in the long run all such memories will be shaped to a significant degree by the new digital technologies and their effects, but they will not be reducible to them. To insist on a radical separation between "real" and virtual memory strikes me as quixotic, if only because anything remembered—whether by lived or by imagined memory—is itself virtual. Memory is always transitory, notoriously unreliable, and haunted by forgetting, in brief, human and social. As public memory it is subject to change—political, generational, individual. It cannot be stored forever, nor can it be secured by monuments. Nor, for that matter, can we rely on digital retrieval systems to guarantee coherence and continuity. If the sense of lived time is being renegotiated in our contemporary cultures of memory, we should not forget that time is not only the past, its preservation and transmission. If we are indeed suffering from a surfeit of memory, we do need to make the effort to distinguish usable pasts from disposable pasts.[18] Discrimination and productive remembering are called for, and mass culture and the virtual media are not inherently irreconcilable with that purpose. Even if amnesia were a by-product of cyberspace, we must not allow the fear of forgetting to overwhelm us. Perhaps it is time to remember the future, rather than simply to worry about the future of memory.

2

Monumental Seduction: Christo in Berlin

Any discussion of monumentality and modernity will inevitably bring to mind the work of Richard Wagner: *The Ring*, the aesthetics of the *Gesamtkunstwerk*, the monumental artist, the history of the Bayreuth festival. But the notion of monumentality that Wagner represents must be located in its concrete nineteenth-century historical, aesthetic, and national context as well as in its political and cultural effects that have come to dominate our understanding of the monumental in general. My purpose is to offer some reflections on the category of the monumental itself, which, it seems to me, is being recoded in the contemporary context of a voracious and ever-expanding memorial culture. My central concern, then, is the issue of the monumental in relation to memory—generational memory, memory in public culture, national memory, memory become stone in architecture—and the specific contemporary context I will address is Germany after unification.

Whereas Germans have been laboring under the reproach of forgetting or repressing their historical past since 1945, critics for some time now have articulated the reverse reproach: inflation of memory. In fact, since the 1980s Germany has engaged in a memory mania of truly monumental proportions. Currently, there are several hundred plans in the works for Holocaust monuments or memorial sites all over Germany. How do we read this obsession with monuments, which in itself is only part of a much larger memory boom that has gripped not just Germany and that is much wider in scope than the focus on the Holocaust would suggest?[1] The questions raised by this conjuncture are invariably political and aesthetic, and central to them is the category of the monumental both in its spatial and, perhaps more important now, in its temporal codifications. We are facing a paradox: monumentalism of built space or monumental tendencies of any other medium continue to be much maligned, but the notion of the monument as memorial or commemorative public event has witnessed a triumphal return. How do we think the relation between monumentality as bigness and the commemorative dimension of the monument? I will relate three events of the summer of 1995 to discuss the fate of monumentality and of monuments in our time: Christo's wrapping of the Reichstag in Berlin, the debate about the planned Berlin monument for the murdered Jews of Europe, and Wagner in Bayreuth.

I

Germany—summer 1995—a few months before the fifth anniversary of national unification. The eighty-fourth Bayreuth Festival opened in July under the motto "redemption through love." An exhibit at Bayreuth's Richard Wagner Museum, subtitled "Richard Wagner and Eroticism," accompanied the *Festspiel* performances of *Tannhäuser*, *Tristan and Isolde*, *The Ring of the Nibelung*, and *Parsifal*, works that, according to Sven Friedrich, the museum's director, represent a very special kind of unity and totality when approached from the angle of eroticism and love. Friedrich described eroticism and love as "symbols of a counterworld" energizing Wagner's dramatic conception of redemption.[2] Bayreuth's need for counterworlds and redemption, it seems, is as strong as ever, but it gained a very specific inflection in 1995.

Germany and redemption—fifty years after. The country was in the grip of a relentless monument mania that may not subside until every square mile has its own monument or memorial site, commemorating not some counterworld of love but the real world of organized destruction and genocide that had adopted Wagner as one of its heroes and prophets. In today's Germany, redemption through memory is the goal. It was particularly striking during the events marking the fiftieth anniversary of the end of the Nazi war of extermination that the discourse of redemption (*Erlö-sung*) had all but replaced the earlier discourses of restitution (*Wiedergut-machung*) and reconciliation (*Versöhnung*). It would seem that the Ger-mans have eagerly appropriated the first part of the old Jewish saying "the secret of redemption is memory" as a strategy for Holocaust management in the 1990s. The most flagrant case: the plan for a gigantic Holocaust memorial, a slanted concrete slab the size of two football fields with the names of millions of victims carved in stone in the heart of Berlin, just north of Hitler's former bunker and thus right on top of the north-south axis that Albert Speer planned to lay between his megalomaniac Great Hall just north of the Brandenburg Gate and Hitler's triumphal arch to the south, which called for the names of the fallen of World War I to be carved in stone. The very site and inscription practice of this prize-winning Holocaust memorial model, which has since been ditched as a result of public outcry, thus appeared to function both as mimesis and cover-up of another site memory, with the requisite monumentality to match the di-mensions of Speer's original plan. It seems striking that a country whose culture has been guided for decades now by a deliberate antifascist anti-monumentalism should resort to monumental dimensions when it comes to public commemoration of the Holocaust for the reunified nation. Something here is out of sync.

But in another perspective, this embrace of the monumental may not be all that surprising. Recalling Robert Musil's observation that there is nothing as invisible as a monument, Berlin—and with it all of this memorial-crazed Germany—is opting for invisibility.[3] The more monu-ments there are, the more the past becomes invisible, and the easier it is to forget: redemption, thus, through forgetting. Many critics have de-scribed Germany's current obsession with monuments and memorials as the not so subtle attempt at *Entsorgung*, the public disposal of radiating historical waste.

Monumental invisibility, at any rate, was at stake during another major cultural event that summer in Berlin: the wrapping of the Reichstag by the artists Christo and Jeanne-Claude. This architecturally mediocre, massive building of 1895 first housed the German parliament in the days of the Wilhelmian Empire and then played a crucial role both in the found-ing and in the toppling of the Weimar Republic, which was proclaimed from its windowsills in 1918 and gutted in the famous Reichstag fire of

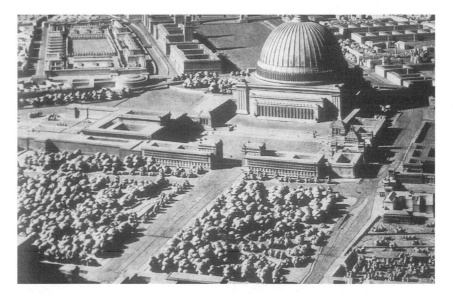

FIGURE 2.1 Albert Speer, Great Hall. Model. Courtesy Architecture Slide Library, Columbia University.

1933, after the Nazis' rise to power. After 1945, it stood as a ruin and a memorial to the failed republic. Having been turned into a museum of recent German history and used as a ceremonial space, it was to resume its symbolic political value with the national unity celebration of October 1990. For two weeks in the summer of 1995, then, this building became temporarily invisible, its invisibility an international media event and popular love fest that celebrated Germany and Berlin as only the fall of the Wall had done six years before. For a brief moment, German history enjoyed the power of the Nibelungs' *Tarnhelm.* The proximity of monumental memory to monumental forgetting was there for everyone to see. Beautification and packaging the past were at stake both in Christo's project and in the award-winning Holocaust monument. Berlin's short-term redemption from history, it seemed, joined Bayreuth's redemption through love in feeding the underlying desire for forgetting.

Predictably enough, some exuberant critics have claimed that by transforming a monumental work of architecture into a gigantic sculpture, Christo and Jeanne-Claude turned a monument of German history into

FIGURE 2.2 Christo, Wrapping of the Reichstag, Berlin (1995). Photo: author.

myth. With such a Wagnerian blending of history, myth, and the monumental, we are no longer surprised to find the project described in a
prominent German art journal as a *Gesamtkunstwerk* that made the German capital into the international capital of art even before the Bonn government moved to Berlin.[4] Such delusional exuberance is matched only by
the insouciance with which Wagner, Adolf Hitler's culture hero, is called
upon to articulate capital claims for Berlin. The polemic could easily be
continued, but its cognitive value, I would suggest, is limited.

What I have argued so far amounts to a symptomatic evil-eye view of
those three cultural events in the summer of 1995: redemption through
love, redemption through memory, redemption through forgetting. No
doubt, some would feel their intellectual posture strengthened by such re-
ductions of complexity. For others, the real questions emerge only now. Is-
n't this whole short-circuited argument, one might ask, structurally reminiscent of a simplistic anti-Wagnerianism that collapses different historical,
political, and aesthetic registers in a causal and teleological model that identifies Wagner's opus entirely with its consequences in the Third Reich?
Furthermore, doesn't this kind of approach create its own good conscience
by being properly antifascist fifty years after the end of the Third Reich, a
kind of political correctness *à l'allemande*? And third, isn't it a kind of
Gesamtkritik that reproduces what it attacks, namely, the discursive totalitarianism that underlies the concept of the *Gesamtkunstwerk* and that mars
so much of Wagner's theoretical and critical writing?

To avoid, then, reproducing what one attacks, a different approach
seems to be called for. After all, most agreed that the polypropylene-
wrapped Reichstag, whose looks oscillated from shining silver in sunlight
to muted gray on cloud-covered days to bluish purple under the spotlights
at night, was serenely and at times uncannily beautiful, its spatial monumentality both dissolved and accentuated by a lightness of being that con-
trasted starkly with the visual memory of the heavy-set, now veiled architecture. Can one really speak of a redemption *from* history when the public
discussions about the history and meaning of this building were never
more intense than in the heated debates that raged in parliament, in the
media, and in the public at large about the merits of Christo's project? The
paradox is that in years past the real Reichstag may have been more invisible—visually and historically—than the veiled building was now. Veiling,
after all, is not the same as packaging. In a larger discursive and public con-

text, Christo's veiling did function as a strategy to make visible, to unveil, to reveal what was hidden when it was visible. Conceptually, the veiling of the Reichstag had another salutary effect: it muted the voice of politics as usual, the memory of speeches from its windows, of the raising of German or Soviet flags on its roof and of the official political rhetoric inside. Thus it opened up a space for reflection and contemplation as well as for memory. The transitoriness of the event itself—the artists refused to prolong the show upon popular demand—was such that it highlighted the temporality and historicity of built space, the tenuous relationship between remembering and forgetting. And the stunningly veiled building itself produced a memory quite different from that marked by the authoritarian inscription above its portal—DEM DEUTSCHEN VOLKE, i.e., given to the German people from on high. The new layer of public memory is that of a genuinely popular event, of thousands of people milling around the building day after day, celebrating a symbol of German democracy in all its fragility and transitoriness. The wrapped Reichstag thus became a monument to democratic culture instead of a demonstration of state power. Even if one should not overestimate this public effect of Christo's project, it does provide a counter-voice to those who have merely criticized the Hollywoodization of avant-gardist art practices or have reduced the whole event to Berlin's desperate need to spruce up its international image.

Thinking about this critical and antimonumental dimension of Christo's project, I was reminded of Wagner's own privileging of the transitory, the ephemeral, the provisional. Thus when he first imagined a performance of *Siegfried*, he wrote to his friend Uhlig that the theater of planks and beams, erected only for the occasion in a meadow near Zurich, would be dismantled after three days and the score burned.[5] In a similar vein, when it came to building the theater in Bayreuth, Wagner always emphasized the provisional nature of the architecture, and Bayreuth as a building turned out indeed to be as antimonumental as Charles Garnier's Paris opera, completed in the same year of 1875, was monumental. Wagner's brief collaboration with the architect Gottfried Semper shipwrecked precisely because Wagner rejected any monumental design for his Festspielhaus, which came to be popularly known as the Bayreuth barn.

If the design of the *Gesamtkunstwerk* can be seen as a monumentalism of the future, then it is to some extent counterbalanced by Wagner's very modern sensibility of the provisionality and ephemerality of institu-

FIGURE 2.3 Christo, Wrapping of the Reichstag. Courtesy Architecture Slide Library, Columbia University.

tionalized art in modernity. Monumental desire and the consciousness of the ephemeral, the transitory, are in uneasy tension in Wagner's mind, a fact that, among other things, may explain Baudelaire's early interest in Wagner's art. The irony, of course, is that Bayreuth became monumental in its own ways and that Wagner's art has become enshrined, institutionalized, and packaged in precisely the ways he found most objectionable in the composer Giacomo Meyerbeer, his nemesis, whose commercial success in Paris Wagner never ceased to deride as decadent and sterile, prostituted and un-German. The success of Bayreuth, however, is no different from what happened to all the subsequent modernisms and avant-gardes as well: incorporation into the culture industry. But there is still a deeper linkage between Wagner and the emergent modernism of his time. The growing recognition since Baudelaire of the provisional, the transitory, the ephemeral, and, yes, the fashionable as key parameters of modernity generates at the opposing end of a tension-filled axis the desire for lasting monumentality, what Paul Eluard called, in an untranslatable phrase, "le dur désir de durer." In Wagner, the anxiety produced by this tension results in a paranoid aggressive streak that couples insight into the transitoriness of art with images of ruin, death, and destruction. The pressures of the transitory affect the monumental itself: the only monument that counts is the one already imagined as ruin. I will come back a little later to this question of a monumentalism of destruction in Wagner.

My main point here is a simple one. Against the gesture and rhetoric of a *Gesamtkritik* that simplistically identifies Wagner's music drama with a typical nineteenth-century monumentalism, it is important to hold on to such ambiguities and contradictions. No doubt, Christo's project, too, had its own monumentality, an extremely seductive one at that which, however, had nothing to do with death and destruction. It was exactly the monumentality of the wrapped Reichstag that raised theoretical questions in my mind about "the monumental" as an aesthetic and a political category. To what extent can the monumentality of the planned Berlin Holocaust Memorial be equated with the monumentality of Speer's architectural phantasmagoria? Is either project similar to the kind of monumental effect Christo achieved by wrapping the Reichstag or to the monumentalism of Wagnerian music drama and its conceptualization? To what extent is the monumental a hidden dimension within modernism itself? Why is it that our prevailing notion of monumentality is so one-dimensional and itself immovably monumental that such questions usually do not even emerge? What is it that makes monumentality into such a negative object of desire? Why is it that the reproach "monumental" functions like a death sentence to any further discussion?

II

A brief historical digression may be in order before I turn to the discourse of the monumental in Wagner's programmatic theoretical and critical writings. At stake in those three cultural events and debates of that German summer of 1995 was an aesthetic consensus that reaches from the modernisms of the earlier twentieth century all the way to the various postmodernisms of our own time. The name of this consensus is antimonumentalism. The monumental is aesthetically suspect because it is tied to nineteenth-century bad taste, to kitsch, and to mass culture. It is politically suspect because it is seen as representative of nineteenth-century nationalisms and of twentieth-century totalitarianisms. It is socially suspect because it is the privileged mode of expression of mass movements and mass politics. It is ethically suspect because in its preference for bigness it indulges in the larger-than-human, in the attempt to overwhelm the individual spectator. It is psychoanalytically suspect because it is tied to narcissistic delusions of grandeur and to imaginary wholeness. It is musically suspect because, well, because of Richard Wagner.

In the essay "Leiden und Größe Richard Wagners," Thomas Mann, who, as we know, was attuned to the ambiguities and ambivalences of Wagner's work, talked about Wagner's monumentalizing claims as "bad 19th century."[6] And the monument mania of our own time brings to mind an entry of Walter Benjamin's *Moscow Diary*: "there is hardly a square in Europe whose secret structure was not profaned and impaired over the course of the 19th century by the introduction of a monument."[7] Just as the temporal sensibility of the modernists directed their ire against tradition and the museal, leading them to disparage both the monumental and monumentality, the postmodernists, too, spoke in the name of a proper antimonumentalism when they first attacked modernist architecture in turn as universalizing, hegemonic, and ossified.

For obvious reasons, architecture serves as the primary medium when the reproach of monumentalism is raised, the reproach that a cultural formation has become congealed, ossified, and immobilized. Forgotten, it seems, is the classical trope according to which the geometrical harmonies of architecture echo those of music, a trope that was significantly refurbished in the Romantic period by Hoffmann, Schelling, and Goethe, among others, and was certainly well known to Wagner. The reductively pejorative equation of the monumental with the architectural in our own time results less from modernist skyscrapers than from the architectural phantasmagorias of Hitler and his master architect, Albert Speer, who placed all the emphasis on the overwhelming and terrorizing effects of building as a tool of mass psychology and domination. Thus for a post-1945 sensibility Michel Foucault could claim that what I am calling here monumental seduction represents "the fascism in us all, in our heads and in our everyday behavior, the fascism that causes us to love power, to desire the very thing that dominates and exploits us."[8]

Against this antimonumentalism as an *idée reçue* of the twentieth century that has always played a central role in the discourse of the anti-Wagnerians above and beyond the uses and abuses of Wagner in the

Third Reich, we should remind ourselves that monumentality as an aesthetic category is as historically contingent and unstable as any other aesthetic category. While the monumental may always be big and awesome, with claims to eternity and permanence, differing historical periods obviously have distinct experiences of what overwhelms, and their desire for the monumental will differ both in quality and in quantity. Thus the seductive power of certain forms of nineteenth-century monumentality, tied as they were to the political needs of the national state and the cultural needs of the bourgeoisie, clearly do not match our aesthetic or political sensibilities, but that does not necessarily imply that we are free from monumental seductions per se. Once we focus on the historical specificity of monumentality, I could well imagine arriving at a conclusion that the identification of monumentalism with fascism and the collapsing of the desire for the monumental with masochism and self-annihilation could become legible as itself an historical text rather than as a universal condition or a meta-historical norm.

Only if we historicize the category of monumentality itself can we step out of the double shadow of a kitsch monumentalism of the nineteenth century and the bellicose antimonumentalism of modernism and postmodernism alike. Only then can we ask the question about monumentality in potentially new ways.

III

What, then, of the discourse of the monumental in Wagner? I will focus here on the linkage between monumentalism and the very prominent discourse of architecture in Wagner's programmatic critical and theoretical writings, which I hold to be central to Wagner's overall aesthetic project.

In his brilliant study of Bataille entitled *Against Architecture*, Denis Hollier has pointed out how the search and desire for the monumental in modernity is always the search and desire for origins.[9] Nowhere is this clearer than in the nineteenth century. The search for origins became inevitable once the political, economic, and industrial revolutions had begun to strip away the religious and metaphysical securities of earlier ages. The nineteenth-century discourse of origins was produced by what Georg Lukács later termed "transcendental homelessness" as the *conditio moderna* and to which he opposed the utopia of an integrated civilization. We have come to read this nineteenth-century obsession with origins and their mythic grounding as fulfilling the culturally legitimizing needs of the postrevolutionary bourgeois nation-state in the grip of accelerating modernization. At the same time, as the example of Lukács indicates, the search for origins and a new, emergent culture could also take on an anti-Western, anticapitalist, and antimodern inflection. The obsession with origins and myth was not just reactionary state ideology or its cultural ideological reflection. Its truth, as Adorno argued, was that it demonstrated how nineteenth-century modernity itself, contrary to its liberal and progressive beliefs, remained bound up with the constitutive dialectic of enlightenment and myth. Wagner is a case in point.

To better understand the link among myth, the monumental, and origins, it is important to remember that for the nineteenth century and contrary to our own time, the monumental was first and foremost embodied in the monuments of classical antiquity, monuments transmitted, more often than not, in fragmentary form. Although classical monuments provided European nations with an anchoring in their cultural roots (think of the tyranny of Greece over Germany), the search for national monuments first created the deep national past that differentiated a given culture from both its European and its non-European others. As ever more monuments were unearthed—Schliemann's excavations and the romance of archaeology attached to his name are paradigmatic here—the monument came to guarantee origin and stability as well as depth of time and of space in a rapidly changing world that was experienced as transitory, uprooting, and unstable. And the primary monument in the nineteenth century's admiration for classical and "pre-historic" antiquity was architecture. Thus it was no coincidence that Hegel placed architecture at the very beginnings of art. Monumental architecture especially—think of the cult of obelisks, pyramids, temples, and memorial and burial towers—seemed to guarantee permanence and to provide the desired bulwark against the speed-up of time, the shifting grounds of urban space, and the transitoriness of modern life. Richard Wagner was very much of this nineteenth century, not *against* architecture, like the modernist Bataille, but unhesitatingly *for* it; not *against* origins, but very much in search of them; not in favor of the pleasures of transitoriness and fashion (as Baudelaire was), but violently opposed to them and in pursuit of a new and permanent culture that would bring to fruition what he called the "art-world-historical task" (*kunstweltgeschichtliche*

Aufgabe) of music, a concept hardly imaginable within French modernist discourse.[10] To see art as performing a world-historical mission is indeed a peculiarly German phenomenon that resulted from the overprivileging of art and culture in the process of shaping national identity in a period preceding the formation of the German nation-state. This notion of art's mission anchored Wagner's self-image of the genius called upon by his *Noth* (need) to give the German *Volk* a new culture.

Anyhow, Wagner's conception of art, drama, and music participates in this widespread nineteenth-century imaginary of triumphal architecture, stable origins, and mythic groundings of the nation. At the same time, the ostentatious monumentality of his artistic project, which he laid out most clearly in essays of the late 1840s and early 1850s, took shape against the backdrop of Wagner's vociferous opposition to a certain kind of nineteenth-century monumentalism. His own monumental project of bringing to life the art of the future, an art that would transcend the current stage of decadence and corruption and would be enshrined in the annual *Festspiele* of Bayreuth, was clearly predicated on two assumptions: rejection of timeless classicist norms that fail, in his eyes, to acknowledge the vital temporal and spatial boundedness of all art and, second, rejection of the historicizing architectural styles that he attributed to the corruptions of luxury and fashion. Thus we read in "The Artwork of the Future":

> She [architecture] *reproduces* the buildings which earlier epochs had produced from their felt need of beauty; she pieces together the individual details of these works, according to her wanton fancy, out of a restless longing for alteration, she stitches every national style of building throughout the world into her motley, disconnected botches; in short—she follows the caprice of Fashion whose frivolous laws she needs must make her own because she nowhere hears the call of inner beautiful Necessity.[11]

In its gendered tropes and its modernist put-down of the nineteenth century's obsession with historical styles, this passage can be read as a kind of critique *avant la lettre* of Vienna's Ringstraße, which became so central to the emergence of architectural modernism in Austria a few decades hence. For Wagner as for the fin de siècle Vienna modernists, both forms of the monumental—the classicist and the historicist—failed to do justice to the demands of the present, but Wagner then articulated these demands themselves in a universalizing, monumentalizing rhetoric.

It is easy to see how Wagner's critique of the monumental already anticipated Nietzsche's reflections on monumental history, but it was Nietzsche who, in one of his posthumously published fragments from 1878, first pointed to the underlying contradiction in Wagner's fight against monumentality: "Wagner fights the monumental, but believes in the universally human."[12] In a similarly contradictory way, Wagner uses a universalizing and mythic image of architecture to ground his own claims to an aesthetic monumentality adequate to an emerging new culture, that of the music drama as the new *Gesamtkunstwerk*. For the very notion of the *Gesamtkunstwerk*—this is my claim—is fundamentally architectural.

The metaphor of architecture functions like a leitmotiv in all Wagner's key programmatic texts—"Art and Revolution," "The Artwork of the Future," "Opera and Drama," and "A Communication to my Friends," written at the time he was conceptualizing his tetralogy. Despite his trenchant critique of the monumental and of classicist norms, his primary model for the artwork of the future is Greek tragedy, and the myth of Antigone becomes the founding stone for Wagner's ideology of absolute and redeeming love as the precondition for the collapse of the existing state so dear to Wagner's dreams of a radically new culture. But in a move typical of post-Herderian cultural history, the normative character of Greek tragedy is framed by a historical narrative of decay and rebirth that receives its mid–nineteenth-century spin from a theory of capitalism as decadence, corruption, and pollution of the German *Volk*. This notion of decay and rebirth is articulated in the first pages of "Art and Revolution":

Hand-in-hand with the dissolution of the Athenian State, marched the downfall of Tragedy. As the spirit of *Community* split itself along a thousand lines of egoistic cleavage, so was the *Gesamtkunstwerk* of Tragedy disintegrated into its individual factors. Above the ruins of tragic art was heard the cry of the mad laughter of Aristophanes, the maker of comedies; and, at the bitter end, every impulse of Art stood still before Philosophy, who read with gloomy mien her homilies upon the fleeting stay of human strength and beauty.[13]

Wagner's own monumental claim to rebuild from the ruins of tragedy and to re-create the *Gesamtkunstwerk* against 2,000 years of world history perceived through a Hegelian lens is thus predicated on a world in ruins, not in the future, but in the deep past. If, however, the origin itself is already conceptualized as ruin, it is hard to imagine how the projected future of the *Gesamtkunstwerk* will avoid a similar fate. And then Wagner takes a second step that translates the historical topos of the rise and fall of cultures into a plainly mythic dimension that posits some disastrous ending already in the very act of foundation. In a key passage from *The Artwork of the Future* he compares the ruins of tragedy to the ruins of the tower of Babel:

Just as in the building of the Tower of Babel, when their speech was confounded and mutual understanding made impossible, the nations severed from each other, each one to go its separate way: so, when all national solidarity had split into a thousand egoistic particularities, did the separate arts depart from the proud and heaven-soaring building of Drama, which had lost the inspiring soul of mutual understanding.[14]

The theme of building a new culture and creating the art adequate to the coming age is always predicated in Wagner on destruction and ruins. The discourse of ruins is inscribed into Wagner's project from the beginning and not only since his Schopenhauerian turn, as some would claim. Wagnerian music drama rises programmatically from the ruins of opera, just as the "fullest flower of *pure Human-love*" (a reference to Antigone, Siegmund and Sieglinde, and Siegfried) sprang "amid the ruins of love of sex, of parents, and of siblings."[15] In a letter to Uhlig of November 12, 1851, which mentions the title of the projected tetralogy for the first time, Wagner has this to say about a performance of the *Ring*:

I can only conceive of performing it after the revolution: only the revolution can provide me with the artists and the audience. Inevitably, the next revolution must bring an end to our whole theater business. The theaters must and will all collapse, this is unavoidable.

From their ruins I will then call up what I need: only then will I find what I need. I shall erect a theatre on the banks of the Rhine, and issue invitations to a great dramatic festival. After a year's preparation, I shall produce my complete work in the course of four days. With this production, I will then convey the meaning of this revolution in its noblest sense to the people of the revolution. This audience will understand me; the current audience is unable to.[16]

Thus in late 1851, less than a month before Louis Napoléon's 18th Brumaire, Wagner imagines the future as a Bonapartist aesthetic putsch laced with Bakuninian anarchist desire and reactionary German populism. Just as Louis Napoléon claimed the mantle of his great uncle, Wagner's ambition was to be perceived as a successor to the two towering artists of the preceding period: Goethe and Beethoven. But this reveals precisely the desire for monumentality, a monumentality characterized by an intense inferiority complex toward these predecessors whose achievements Wagner often despaired of matching. Thomas Mann spoke eloquently of Wagner's art as of a "monumentalized . . . dilettantism."[17] But contrary to the monumental works of either Goethe or Beethoven, *Faust* and the *Ninth Symphony* respectively, Wagner's fantasies of the future are always predicated on death, destruction, and disaster, both in his theoretical writings and in his music dramas. The new world promised by Siegfried would rise from the ruins of Valhalla, ruins of a castle of the dead to begin with: architecture as burial site and memorial of heroic death or failure standing at both the beginning and the ending of time. The key function of this vision of monumentality emerges here: it guarantees the presence of the dead without whose sacrifice there can be no new culture. The leitmotiv of architecture in ruins provides mythic closure to Wagner's romantic quest: what is being built is always already a tomb, a memorial to failure and disaster. Wagner's antipathy toward the monumental as classicist norm is grounded in his imaging the monumental as ruin only, for only ruins have permanence. This is where a nineteenth-century discourse of the monument as ruin meets with Albert Speer's ruin theory of architecture, which had the express intent to build in such a way that the greatness of the Third Reich would still be visible in its ruins a thousand years hence. It was the last stage of a Romanticism of ruins in which an originally melancholy and contemplative impulse was transformed into an imperialist project of conquering time and space. Here, too, Wagner appears Janus-faced, looking both backward to Romanticism and forward to a violent, engulfing future. The simultaneity of the desire for permanence and the anticipation of destruction is reminiscent of Elias Canetti's reflection on Hitler's hesitation over whether or not to destroy Paris. In *Masses and Power*, Canetti read Hitler's dilemma as the twofold delight in permanence and destruction characteristic of the paranoiac. Of course, Wagner saw himself as the "plenipotentiary of downfall,"[18] and in another letter to Uhlig of October 22, 1850, shortly after publishing "Judaism in Music," he wrote: "In total calm and without any hoax I assure you that the only revolution I believe in, is the one that begins with the burning down of Paris."[19]

In the end Paris was not burned, not even by the Nazis. But the German state has collapsed four times in one century. And yet, fortunately, the new monumental culture Wagner intended to found with his music drama on the ruins of the state never arrived, nor did the new Aristophanes who would sit crying and laughing atop the ruins of Wagner's *Gesamtkunstwerk*. Instead, Bayreuth as an exemplary sector of the international opera industry is well and alive. We have the *Ring of the Nibelung* as a comic book and the program-note description of a 1980s Met production as *Dallas on the Rhine*. We may not need another Aristophanes, and that may be just as well.

IV

But what then of the monumental today? Our own way of enjoying an aesthetics of monumentality—if we can bring ourselves to admit that in some forms the monumental can be enjoyed and must not be rejected at all costs—seems to me adequately embodied in Christo's wrapping of the Reichstag: a monumentality that can do without permanence and without destruction, one that is fundamentally informed by the modernist spirit of a fleeting and transitory epiphany, but that is no less memorable or monumental for it. The project's monumentality was that of a great cultural event disseminated and memorialized by the media, an event that was monumental and anti-monumental at the same time. But the Christo project was an art event, a nomadic installation. It was not designed as permanent built space but rather as its temporary dissolution. Thus its celebration begs the question of whether a monumental architecture is possible today, or even desirable.

This brings me to a final reflection that opens up another set of questions inherent in Christo's project and important to the issue of monumentality in our culture. In 1943 in New York, the painter Fernand Léger, the architect and town planner José Luis Sert, and the historian Siegfried Giedeon called for a new monumentality in architecture. In their jointly authored programmatic statement entitled "Nine Points on Monumentality," they argued against the pseudo-monumentality of the nineteenth century as much as against the pure functionalism of the Bauhaus and the International Style.[20] Their theses are informed by the democratic conviction that there is a legitimate desire for monumental public space. Monuments are seen as expressing the highest cultural needs of a people, and thus the authors lament the devaluation of monumentality within modernism. Today, their manifesto reads like a last-ditch attempt to reinscribe a democratic monumentality into the modernist project, an impetus that can be historicized as belonging squarely within the New Deal era. The fact that its rhetoric now sounds hollow is testimony to the further decline of monumental public space in the past decades. Neither Rem Koolhaas's recent triumphalism of extra large in his book *SMLXL*, with its celebration of bigness in city planning, nor the few successful new public monuments such as the Vietnam Memorial in Washington can hide the fact that we are waiting in vain for the resurrection of a public monumentality. Perhaps the wrapping of the Reichstag, which can now be seen only in reproducible media images on postcards, T-shirts, coffee cups, and the Internet, is symptomatic of the fate of the monumental in our postmodern times: it has migrated from the real into the image, from the material into the immaterial, and ultimately into the digitized computer bank.

As so often in media politics, the Nazis had the right instinct when they mass-distributed images of Speer's models in the form of postcards. The monumental effect of architecture could just as easily, perhaps even better, be achieved, say, by a high-angle, totalizing *image* of architecture. No need even to build the real thing. For years after the war, many Germans mistakenly believed that Speer's Berlin projects had actually been built and then destroyed in the last stages of the war.

Thus fifty and some years later, our own monumental seduction may be no longer tied up with real built space at all, certainly not with the mammoth shopping malls in the middle of nowhere, nor with international airports and their mass circulation of people and commodities, both of which are physically uncoupled from the traditional site of public space: the living city. No wonder, then, that some will look for the new public space on the Internet, our very own monumental seduction that holds the promise of conquering both time and space and that gives new meaning to McLuhan's phantasm of an electronically unified global culture. Monumentality today may all be in cyberspace and the information highway. The Germans, at any rate, in seamless and oblivious continuity with another monumental Nazi project—the building of the Autobahn—call it Infobahn, and Deutsche Telekom, in a recent ad in the *New York Times*, has described it without hesitation as "the fast lane to the future." Monumentality is alive and well. We may in fact have to consider a monumentality of miniaturization, for the world wide web is in principle the most gigantic undertaking of our age, as promising to some and threatening to others as any monumentalism has ever been. Significantly, however, the Telekom ad cannot do without a national monument: it enlists the Brandenburg Gate as a trademark for "made in Germany." Whether the information traffic to the future will be in the fast lane or whether it will generate brain jam on a monumental scale remains to be seen.

Only the future will tell whether it was worth being seduced.

3

The Voids of Berlin

I

Eight years after the fall of the Wall, seven years after the unification of East and West Germany, and just a couple of years before the final transfer of the national government from Bonn to the city on the Spree, Berlin is a city text frantically being written and rewritten. As Berlin has left behind its heroic and propagandistic role as flash point of the Cold War and struggles to imagine itself as the new capital of a reunited nation, the city has become something like a prism through which we can focus issues of contemporary urbanism and architecture, national identity and statehood, historical memory and forgetting. Architecture has always been deeply invested in the shaping of political and national identities, and the rebuilding of Berlin as capital of Germany gives us significant clues to the state of the German nation after the fall of the Wall and about the ways it projects its future.

As a literary critic I am naturally attracted to the notion of the city as text, of reading a city as a conglomeration of signs. Mindful of Italo Calvino's marvelously suggestive *Invisible Cities*, we know how real and imaginary spaces commingle in the mind to shape our notions of specific cities. No matter where we begin our discussion of the city of signs— whether with Victor Hugo's reading Paris in *Notre Dame de Paris* as a book written in stone, with Alfred Döblin's attempt, in *Berlin Alexanderplatz*, to create a montage of multiple city discourses jostling against each other like passers-by on a crowded sidewalk, with Walter Benjamin's notion of the flaneur reading urban objects in commemorative meditation, with Robert Venturi's upbeat emphasis on architecture as image, meaning, and communication, with Roland Barthes's city semiotics of the *Empire of Signs*, with Thomas Pynchon's TV-screen city, or with Jean Baudrillard's aesthetic transfiguration of an immaterial New York—a few things should be remembered: The trope of the city as book or as text has existed as long as we have had a modern city literature. There is nothing particularly novel or postmodern about it. On the other hand, one may want to ask why this notion of the city as sign and text assumed such critical mass in the architectural discourse of the 1970s and 1980s, arguably the high time of an architectural obsession with semiotics, rhetorics, and codings that underwrote much of the debate about architectural postmodernism. Whatever the explanation may be—and surely, there is no one simple answer to this question—it seems clear that today this interest in the city as sign, as text, is waning in much architectural discourse and practice, both of which have by and large turned against an earlier fascination with literary and linguistic models, no doubt at least partially as a result of the new image-graphing technologies offered by ever more powerful computers. The notion of the city as sign, however, is as pertinent as before, though perhaps more now in a pictorial and imagistic rather than a textual sense. But this shift from script to image comes with a significant reversal. Put bluntly: The discourse of the city as text in the 1970s was primarily a critical discourse involving architects, literary critics, theorists, and philosophers bent on exploring and creating the new vocabularies of urban space after modernism. The current discourse of the city as image is one of "city fathers," developers, and politicians trying to increase revenue from mass tourism, conventions, and office or commercial rental. Central to this new kind of urban politics are aesthetic spaces for cultural consumption, megastores and blockbuster museal events, *Festspiele* and spectacles of all kinds, all intended to lure that new species of the city-tourist, the urban vacationer or even the metropolitan marathoner, who has replaced the older leisurely flaneur. The flaneur, though always something of an outsider in his city, was still figured as a dweller rather than as a traveler on the move. But today it is the tourist rather than the flaneur to whom the new city culture wants to appeal—even as it fears the tourist's underside, the displaced and illegal migrant.

There is a clear downside to *this* notion of the city as sign and image in our global culture, nowhere as visible to me as in a recent front-page article in the *New York Times* in which the paper's art critic celebrated the newly Disneyfied and theme-parked Times Square as the ultimate example of a commercial billboard culture that has now, in this critic's skewed view, become indistinguishable from real art.[1] One can only hope that the transformation of Times Square from a haven for hustlers, prostitutes, and junkies into a pop art installation will not presage the wholesale transformation of Manhattan into a museum, a process already far advanced in some older European cities.

This brings me back to Berlin, a city justly famous for its glorious museum collections, but, owing mainly to its decenteredness and vast extension, much less liable to turn into an urban museum space such as the centers of Rome, Paris, or even London have become in recent decades. Thus it is no big surprise to me that after an upsurge in the early 1990s, tourism to Berlin is significantly down. This slump may of course have something to do with the fact that Berlin is currently the most energized site for new urban construction anywhere in the Western world: enormously exciting for people interested in architecture and urban transformation, but for most others mainly an insufferable mess of dirt, noise, and traffic jams. Once all this construction has been completed, this is the hope, Berlin will take its rightful place as a European capital next to its more glamorous competitors. But will it? After all, Berlin is in significant ways different from other Western European capitals, in terms of its history as capital and as an industrial center as well as in terms of its building substance. And the fact that the city is now caught between the pressures of this new urban image politics and the more general crisis of architectural developments at the millennium's end makes any such hope appear simply misplaced if not deluded. I do think that Berlin is *the* place to study how this new emphasis on the city as cultural sign, combined with its role as capital and the pressures of large-scale developments, prevents creative alternatives and thus represents a false start into the twenty-first century. In short, Berlin may be well on the way to squandering a unique chance.

II

There is perhaps no other major Western city that bears the marks of twentieth-century history as intensely and self-consciously as Berlin. This city text has been written, erased, and rewritten throughout that violent

FIGURE 3.1 Philip Johnson Haus near former Checkpoint Charlie (1996).
Photo: author.

century, and its legibility relies as much on visible markers of built space as
on images and memories repressed and ruptured by traumatic events. Part
palimpsest, part *Wunderblock*, Berlin now finds itself in a frenzy of future
projections and, in line with the general memorial obsessions of the 1990s,
in the midst of equally intense debates about how to negotiate its Nazi and
communist pasts, now that the safe dichotomies of the Cold War have
vanished. The city is obsessed with architectural and planning issues, a debate that functions like a prism refracting the pitfalls of urban development at this turn of the century. All of this in the midst of a government-
and corporation-run building boom of truly monumental proportions.
Nothing less is the goal than to create the capital of the twenty-first century, but this vision finds itself persistently haunted by the past.

Berlin as text remains first and foremost historical text, marked as
much, if not more, by absences as by the visible presence of its past, from
prominent ruins such as the Gedächtniskirche at the end of the famous
Kurfürstendamm to World War II bullet and shrapnel marks on many of
its buildings. It was in the months after the collapse of the East German
state that our sensibility for the past of this city was perhaps most acute, a

FIGURE 3.2 Former Checkpoint Charlie with imitation Statue of Liberty (1995).
Courtesy Elisabeth Felicella.

city that for so long had stood in the dead eye of the storm of politics in
this century. Empire, war and revolution, democracy, fascism, Stalinism,
and the Cold War all were played out here. Indelibly etched into our
memory is the idea of Berlin as the capital site of a discontinuous, ruptured
history, of the collapse of four successive German states; Berlin as ground
of literary expressionism and the revolt against the old order; Berlin as epi-
center of the vibrant cultural avant-gardism of Weimar and its elimination
by Nazism; Berlin as command center of world war and the Holocaust;
and, finally, Berlin as symbolic space of the East-West confrontation of the
nuclear age with American and Soviet tanks staring each other down at
Checkpoint Charlie, which is now being turned into an American business
center watched over, temporarily, by a towering photographic cutout of
Philip Johnson and a shrunken, gilded Statue of Liberty placed atop the
former East German watchtower.

   If, at that confusing and exhilarating time after the fall of the Wall,
Berlin seemed saturated with memories, the years since then have also
taught us multiple lessons about the politics of willful forgetting: the im-
posed and often petty renaming of streets in East Berlin that were given

back their presocialist, and often decidedly antisocialist, cast, the dismantling of monuments to socialism, the absurd debate about tearing down the GDR's Palace of the Republic to make room for a rebuilding of the Hohenzollern palace, and so forth. This was not just tinkering with the communist city text. It was a strategy of power and humiliation, a final burst of Cold War ideology, pursued via a politics of signs, much of it wholly unnecessary and with predictable political fallout in an East German population that felt increasingly deprived of its life history and of its memories of four decades of separate development. Even though not all the plans to dismantle monuments and to rename streets came to fruition, the damage was done. GDR nostalgia and an upsurge in popularity for the revamped Communist Party (PDS) were the inevitable political results, even among many in the younger generation who had been active in the opposition to the state in the 1980s.

Forgetting is equally privileged in an official ad campaign of 1996, literally written all over the city: BERLIN WIRD—BERLIN BECOMES. But "becomes what"? Instead of a proper object, we get a verbal void. This phrasing may reflect wise precaution, for in the current chaos of public planning, backdoor scheming, and contradictory politicking, with many architectural developments (Spreeinsel and Alexanderplatz among them) still hanging in the air and their feasibility and financing insecure, nobody seems to know exactly what Berlin will become. But the optimistic subtext of the ellipsis is quite clear, and radically opposed to Karl Scheffler's 1910 lament that it is the tragic destiny of Berlin "forever to become and never to be."[2] Too much of the current construction and planning actually lacks the very dynamism and energy of turn-of-the-century Berlin that Scheffler, ever the cultural pessimist, lamented. Since much of central Berlin in the mid-1990s is a gigantic construction site, a hole in the ground, a void, there are ample reasons to emphasize the void rather than to celebrate Berlin's current state of becoming.

III

The notion of Berlin as a void is more than a metaphor, and it is not just a transitory condition. It does carry historical connotations. Already in 1935, the Marxist philosopher Ernst Bloch, in his *Erbschaft dieser Zeit*, described life in Weimar Berlin as "functions in a void."[3] He was referring to the vacuum left by the collapse of an earlier, nineteenth-century bourgeois culture, which had found its spatial expression in the heavy ornamental stone architecture of Berlin's unique apartment buildings, the pejoratively called *Mietkasernen* (rent barracks), with their multiple wings in the back, their so-called *Hinterhäuser* enclosing inner courtyards accessible from the street only through tunnel-like archways. The post–World War I vacuum was filled by a functionalist and, to Bloch, insubstantial culture of distraction: Weimar modernism, the movie palaces, the six-day bicycle races, the new modernist architecture, the glitz and glamour of the so-called stabilization phase before the 1929 crash. Bloch's phrase "functions in the void" also articulated the insight that in the age of monopoly capitalism, built city space could no longer command the representative functions of an earlier age. As Brecht put it in those same years, when he discussed the need for a new, postmimetic realism: reality itself had become functional, thus requiring entirely new modes of representation.[4]

A little over a decade later, it was left to fascism to transform Berlin into the literal void that was the landscape of ruins of 1945. Especially in the center of Berlin, British and American bombers had joined forces with Albert Speer's wrecking crews to create a tabula rasa for Germania, the renamed capital of a victorious Reich. And the creation of voids did not stop then; it continued through the 1950s under the heading of *Sanierung*, when entire quarters of the old Berlin were razed to make room for the simplistic versions of modern architecture and planning characteristic of the times. The major construction project of the postwar period, the Wall, needed another void, that of the no-man's-land and the minefields that wound their way through the very center of the city and held its Western part in a tight embrace.

All of West Berlin itself always appeared as a void on Eastern European maps: West Berlin of the Cold War as the hole in the Eastern European cheese. Likewise weather maps on West German television for a long time represented the GDR as an absence, a blank space surrounding the Frontstadt Berlin, the capitalist cheese in the real existing void.

When the Wall came down, Berlin added another chapter to its narrative of voids, a chapter that brought back shadows of the past and spooky revenants. For a couple of years, this very center of Berlin, the threshold between the Eastern and the Western parts of the city, was a seventeen-acre wasteland that extended from the Brandenburg Gate down to Potsdamer and Leipziger Platz, a wide stretch of dirt, grass, and remnants of former pavement under a big sky that seemed even bigger given

FIGURE 3.3 Wall area between Leipziger Platz and Brandenburg Gate. Courtesy Architecture Slide Library, Columbia University.

the absence of any high-rise skyline so characteristic of this city. Berliners called it affectionately their "wonderful city steppes," their "prairie of history."[5] It was a haunting space, crisscrossed by a maze of footpaths going nowhere. One slight elevation marked the remnants of the bunker of Hitler's SS guard, which after having been reopened once the Wall came down was soon sealed shut again by the city authorities to avoid making it into a site of neo-Nazi pilgrimage. Walking across this space that had been a mined no-man's-land framed by the Wall and that now served occasionally as a staging site for rock concerts and other transitory cultural attrac-

FIGURE 3.4 Albert Speer, North-South Axis. Model. Courtesy Architecture Slide Library, Columbia University.

FIGURE 3.5 Installation in the void left by the dismantling of the Wall (1991).
Photo: author.

tions, I could not help remembering that this tabula rasa had once been
the site of Hitler's Reichskanzlei and the space to be occupied by Speer's
megalomaniac north-south axis with the Great Hall in the north and
Hitler's triumphal arch in the south, the power center of the empire of a
thousand years, all to be completed by 1950.

In the summer of 1991, when most of the Wall had already been removed, auctioned off, or sold to tourists in bits and pieces, the area was
studded with the Wall's steel rods left by the *Mauerspechte*, the wall peck-
ers, and decorated with colorful triangular paper leaves that were blowing
and rustling in the wind: they powerfully marked the void as second nature and as memorial.

The installation increased the uncanny feeling: a void saturated with
invisible history, with memories of architecture both built and unbuilt. It
gave rise to the desire to leave it as it was, the memorial as empty page right
in the center of the reunified city, the center that was and always had been
at the same time the very threshold between the eastern and western parts
of the city, the space that now, in yet another layer of signification, seemed

to be called upon to represent the invisible "wall in the head" that still separated East and West Germans and that was anticipated by the novelist Peter Schneider long before the actual wall came down.[6]

Since then, the rebuilding of this empty center of Berlin has become a major focus of all discussions about the Berlin of tomorrow. With the new government quarter in the bend of the river Spree next to the Reichstag in the north and the corporate developments at Potsdamer and Leipziger Platz at the southern end of this space, Berlin will indeed gain a new center of corporate and governmental power.

But how important should the city center be for the cities of the future? After all, the city as center and the centered city are themselves in question today. Bernard Tschumi puts it well when he asks,

FIGURE 3.6 Potsdamer Platz around 1930. Courtesy Architecture Slide Library, Columbia University.

how can architecture whose historical role was to generate the appearance of stable images (monuments, order, etc.) deal with today's culture of the disappearance of unstable images (twenty-four-image-per-second cinema, video, and computer-generated images)?[7]

For some world wide web surfers and virtual city flaneurs, the built city itself has become obsolete. Others, however, like Saskia Sassen, the New York urbanist, or Dieter Hoffmann-Axthelm, a well-known Berlin architecture critic, have argued persuasively that it is precisely the growth of global telecommunications and the potential dispersal of population and resources that have created a new logic for concentration in what Sassen calls the global city.[8] Indeed, the city as center is far from becoming obsolete. But as a center, the city is increasingly affected and structured by our culture of media images. In the move from the city as regional or national center of production to the city as international center of communications, media, and services, the very image of the city itself becomes central to its success in a globally competitive world. From New York's new Times Square with its culture industry giants Disney and Bertelsmann and with its ecstasies of flashing commercial signage, to Berlin's new Potsdamer Platz, with Sony, Mercedes, and Brown Boveri, visibility equals success.

Not surprisingly, then, the major concern with developing and rebuilding key sites in the heart of Berlin seems to be image rather than usage, attractiveness for tourists and official visitors rather than heterogeneous living space for Berlin's inhabitants, erasure of memory rather than its imaginative preservation. The new architecture is to enhance the desired image of Berlin as capital and global metropolis of the twenty-first century, as a hub between Eastern and Western Europe, and as a center of corporate presence, however limited that presence may in the end turn out to be. But ironically, the concern with Berlin's image, foremost on the minds of politicians who desire nothing so much as to increase Berlin's ability to attract corporations and tourists, clashes with what I would describe as the fear of an architecture of images.

IV

This tension has produced a very sharp debate in which the battle lines are firmly entrenched between the defenders of a national tradition and the advocates of a contemporary high-tech global architecture. The traditionalists champion a local and national concept of urban culture that they call "critical reconstruction."[9] Its representatives, such as Hans Stimmann, the city's director of building from 1991 to 1996, and Victor Lampugnani, former director of Frankfurt's Museum of Architecture, call for a new simplicity that seems to aim at a mix of Karl Friedrich Schinkel's classicism and Peter Behrens's once daring modernism, with Heinrich Tessenow as a moderate modernist thrown in to secure an anti–avantgardist and anti–Weimar politics of traditionalism. Berlin must be Berlin, they say. Identity is at stake. But this desired identity is symptomatically dominated by pre–World War I architecture, the *Mietkaserne,* and the notion of the once again popular traditional neighborhood, affectionately called the *Kiez.* In the late 1970s, the *Kiez* emerged as counterculture in run-down, close-to-the-Wall quarters like Kreuzberg where squatters occupied and restored decaying housing stock. In the 1980s, it was embraced by the city's mainstream preservation efforts. Now, it dictates key parameters of the new architectural conservatism. Forgotten are the architectural and planning experiments of the 1920s, the great Berlin estates of Martin Wagner and Bruno Taut. Forgotten or rather repressed is the architecture of the Nazi period, of which Berlin, after all, still harbors significant examples, from the Olympic Stadium to Göring's aviation ministry near Leipziger Platz. Ignored and to be quickly forgotten is the architecture of the GDR, which many would just like to commit in its entirety to the wrecking ball—from the *Stalinallee* all the way to satellite housing projects like Marzahn or Hohenschönhausen. What we have instead is a strange mix of an originally leftist *Kiez* romanticism and a nineteenth-century vision of the neighborhood divided into small parcels, as if such structures could become prescriptive for the rebuilding of the city as a whole. But this is precisely what bureaucrats like Hans Stimmann and theorists like Dieter Hoffmann-Axthelm have in mind with critical reconstruction. Prescriptions such as city block building, traditional window facades, a uniform height of twenty-two meters (the ritualistically invoked *Traufhöhe*), and building in stone are vociferously defended against all evidence that such traditionalism is wholly imaginary. Building in stone, indeed, at a time when the most stone you'd get is a thin stone veneer covering the concrete skeleton underneath.

There is not much of interest to say about the other, the corporate side, of the debate. Here we have international high tech, facade ecstasy, preference for mostly banal high-rises, and floods of computer-generated imagery to convince us that we need to go with the future. But this dichotomy of Stone Age vs. cyber age is misleading: the fight is over image and image alone on both sides of the issue. The new nationally coded simplicity is just as image-driven as the image ecstasies of the high-tech camp, except that it posits banal images of a national past against equally banal images of a global future. The real Berlin of today, its conflicts and aspirations, remains a void in a debate that lacks imagination and vision.

Take Hans Stimmann and Victor Lampugnani. Lampugnani disapproves of "easy pictures . . . superficial sensation . . . tormented lightness . . . wild growth . . . nosy new interpretation."[10] Stimmann in turn protests that "Learning from Las Vegas" is out of place in a central European city, a programmatic statement as much directed against postmodernism in architecture as it is quite blatantly anti-American in the tradition of conservative German *Kulturkritik*.[11] But this attack on a twenty-five-year-old founding text of postmodern architecture and its reputed image politics is strangely out of place and out of time. Las Vegas postmodernism has been defunct for some time, and nobody has ever suggested that Berlin should become casino city. The hidden object of Stimmann's moralizing protest is Weimar Berlin. For Berlin in the 1920s, we must remember, defined its modernity as quintessentially "American": Berlin as a "Chicago on the Spree," and as such different from older European capitals and different also from the Berlin of the Wilhelmian Empire. The embrace of America was an embrace of pragmatic technological modernity, functionalism, mass culture, and democracy. America then offered images of the new, but memories of Weimar architecture—Erich Mendelsohn, Walter Gropius and the Bauhaus, Bruno Taut, Martin Wagner, Hannes Meyer, Mies van der Rohe—simply do not figure in the current debates about architecture in Berlin. In their antimodernism, the conservatives themselves have gone postmodern. Small wonder then that Stimmann's preference for "critical reconstruction" is itself primarily concerned with image and advertising: the image of built space creating a sense of traditional identity for Berlin, whose voids must be filled, and the more intangible, yet economically decisive international image of the city in an age of global service economies, urban tourism, cultural competition, and new concentrations of wealth and power. But the desired image is decidedly pre-1914. The critical reconstructionists fantasize about a second *Gründerzeit* analo-

FIGURE 3.7 Potsdamer Platz construction site with INFO BOX (1995). Courtesy Elisabeth Felicella.

gous to the founding years of the Second Reich after the Franco-Prussian War. Never mind that the gold rush of the first *Gründerzeit* quickly collapsed with the crash of 1873 and the beginning of a long-term depression.

The issue in central Berlin, to use Venturi/Scott Brown/Izenour's by now classical postmodern terms from *Learning from Las Vegas* in this very different context, is about how best to decorate the corporate and governmental sheds to better attract international attention: not the city as multiply coded text to be filled with life by its dwellers and its readers, but the city as image and design in the service of displaying power and profit. This underlying goal has paradigmatically come to fruition in a project on Leipziger Platz called INFO BOX, a huge red box on black stilts with window fronts several stories high and with an open-air roof terrace for panoramic viewing.

This INFO BOX, attraction to some five thousand visitors per day, was built in 1995 as a temporary installation to serve as a viewing site onto the construction wasteland studded with building cranes that surrounds it. With its multimedia walls, sound rooms, and interactive computers, it serves as an exhibition and advertising site for the corporate developments by Mercedes, Sony, and the A+T Investment Group on Leipziger and Potsdamer Platz. As cyber flaneur in "Virtual Berlin 2002," you can enjoy a fly-through through a computer simulation of the new Potsdamer and Leipziger Platz developments or arrive by ICE at the future Lehrter Bahnhof. You can watch the construction site on a wraparound amphitheatrical screen inside, while listening to an animated Disneyfied Berlin sparrow deliver the proud narrative cast in a typically street-smart, slightly lower-class Berlin intonation. Or you can admire plaster casts of the major architects—the cult of the master builder is alive and well as simulacrum, all the more so as architects have become mere appendages in today's world of urban development. More image box than info box, this space offers the ultimate paradigm of the many *Schaustellen* (viewing and spectacle sites), which the city mounted in the summer of 1996 at its major *Baustellen* (construction sites). Berlin as a whole advertised itself as *Schaustelle* with the slogan "*Bühnen, Bauten, Boulevards*" (stages, buildings, boulevards) and mounted a cultural program including over two hundred guided tours of construction sites, eight hundred hours of music, acrobatics, and pantomime on nine open-air stages throughout the summer. From void, then, to mise-en-scène and to image, images in the void: *Berlin wird* . . . Berlin becomes image.

Is it only perverse to compare the gaze from the INFO BOX's terrace onto the construction wasteland of Potsdamer Platz to that other gaze we all remember, the gaze from the primitive elevated wooden (later metal) platform erected near the Wall west of Potsdamer Platz to allow Western visitors to take a long look eastward across the death strip as emblem of communist totalitarianism? It would be perverse only if one were simply to equate the two sites. And yet the memory of that other viewing platform will not go away as it shares with the INFO BOX a certain obnoxious triumphalism: the political triumphalism of the Free World in the Cold War now having been replaced by the triumphalism of the free market in the age of corporate globalization.

Perhaps the box and the screen *are* our future. After all, the completed developments on Friedrichstraße, that major commercial artery crossing Unter den Linden, look frighteningly similar to their former computer simulations, with one major difference: what appeared airy, sometimes even elegant, and generously spacious in the simulations now looks oppressively monumental, massive, and forbidding, especially when experienced under the leaden Berlin skies in midwinter. Call it the revenge of the real. In addition, some of the new fancy malls on Friedrichstraße, meant to compete with the KaDeWe (*Kaufhaus des Westens*) and the shopping area on and near Kurfürstendamm, are not very successful, and Berlin already has surplus office space for rent as more is being built day by day. Thus my fear for the future of Potsdamer and Leipziger Platz: just as the INFO BOX immobilizes the flaneur facing the screen, the tight corporate structures, despite their gesturing toward public spaces and piazzas, will encage and confine their visitors rather than create anything like the open, mobile, and multiply coded urban culture that once characterized this pivotal traffic hub between the eastern and western parts of the city. There is good reason to doubt whether Helmut Jahn's happy plastic tent hovering above the central plaza of the Sony development will make up for the loss of urban life that these developments will inevitably entail.

V

Looking at the forces and pressures that currently shape the new Berlin, one may well fear that the ensemble of architectural solutions proposed may represent the worst start into the twenty-first century one could imagine for this city. Many of the major construction projects, it seems, have been designed against the city rather than for it. Some of them look like corporate spaceships reminiscent of the conclusion of *Close Encounters of the Third Kind.* The trouble is, they are here to stay. The void in the center of Berlin will have been filled. But memories of that haunting space from the months and years after the Wall came down will linger. The one architect who understood the nature of this empty space in the center of Berlin was Daniel Libeskind, who, in 1992, made the following proposal:

Rilke once said that everything is already there. We only must see it and protect it. We must develop a feel for places, streets, and houses which need our support. Take the open area at the Potsdamer Platz. I suggest a wilderness, one kilometer long, within which everything can stay as it is. The street simply ends in the bushes. Wonderful. After all, this area is the result of today's divine natural law: nobody wanted it, nobody planned it, and yet it is firmly implanted in all our minds. And there in our minds, this image of the Potsdamer Platz void will remain for decades. Something like that cannot be easily erased, even if the whole area will be developed.[12]

Of course, what Libeskind describes tongue-in-cheek as "today's divine natural law" is nothing but the pressure of history that created this void called Potsdamer Platz in the first place: the saturation bombings of 1944–45, which left little of the old Potsdamer Platz structures standing; the building of the Wall in 1961, which required a further clearing of the area; the tearing down of the wall in 1989, which made this whole area between the Brandenburg Gate and Potsdamer Platz into that prairie of history that Berliners quickly embraced. It was a void filled with history and memory, all of which will be erased (I'm less sanguine about the power of memory than Libeskind) by the new construction.

In light of Libeskind's own architectural project, however, which is crucially an architecture of memory, even his suggestion to leave the void as it was in the early 1990s was not just romantic and impractical. For Libeskind gave architectural form to another void that haunts Berlin, the historical void left by the Nazi destruction of Berlin's thriving Jewish life and culture. A discussion of Libeskind's museum project, arguably the single most interesting new building in Berlin, is appropriate here not only because it gives a different inflection to the notion of Berlin as void in relation to memory and to history, but because, however indirectly, it raises the issue of German national identity and the identity of Berlin. While all the other major building sites in Berlin today are inevitably haunted by the past, only Libeskind's building attempts to articulate memory and our relationship to it in its very spatial organization.

VI

In 1989, just a few months before the Wall cracked, Daniel Libeskind surprisingly won a competition to build the expansion of the Berlin Museum with the Jewish Museum, as it is awkwardly, and yet appropriately, called.

The Berlin Museum was founded in 1962 as a local history museum for the western part of the divided city, clearly a reaction to the building of the Wall, which had made the former local history museum, the Märkisches Museum, inaccessible. Since the mid-1970s, the Berlin Museum has had a Jewish section that documents the role of German Jewry in the history of Berlin. With the new expansion, the museum was to consist of three parts: general history of Berlin from 1870 to today, Jewish history in

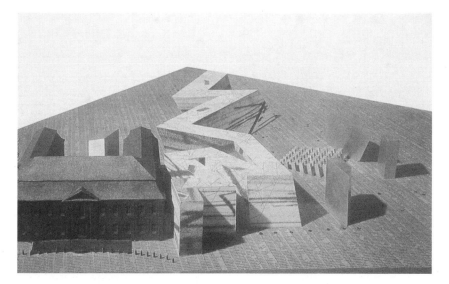

FIGURE 3.8 Berlin Museum with the Jewish Museum. Model. Courtesy Büro Daniel Libeskind.

Berlin, and an in-between space dedicated to the theme of Jews in society, which would articulate the relations and crossovers between the other two components. Libeskind's proposal was as architecturally daring as it was conceptually persuasive, and even though multiple resistances—political, aesthetic, economic—had to be overcome, the museum has been built and celebrated its opening in September 2001.

The expansion sits next to the old Berlin Museum, a baroque palace that used to house the Berlin Chamber Court before it became a museum in 1962. The old and the new parts are apparently disconnected, and the only entrance to the expansion building is underground from the old building. Libeskind's structure has often been described as zigzag, as lightning, or, because it is to house a Jewish collection, as a fractured Star of David. He himself has called it "Between the Lines."

The ambiguity between an architecturally spatial and a literary meaning (one reads between the lines) is intended, and it suggests the conceptual core of the project. The basic structure of the building is found in the relation between two lines, one straight but broken into pieces, divided into fragments, the other multiply bent, contorted, but potentially going

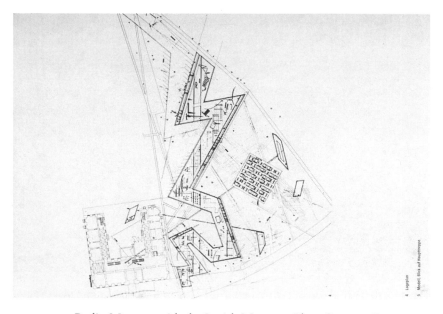

FIGURE 3.9 Berlin Museum with the Jewish Museum. Plan. Courtesy Büro Daniel Libeskind.

on ad infinitum. Architecturally this longitudinal axis translates into a thin slice of empty space that crosses the path of the zigzag structure at each intersection and that reaches from the bottom of the building to the top. It is sealed to the exhibition halls of the museum. It cannot be entered, but it is accessible to view from the small bridges that cross it at every level of the building: it is a view into an abyss extending downward and upward at the same time. Libeskind calls it the void.

This fractured and multiply interrupted void functions like a spine to the building. It is both conceptual and literal. And clearly, it signifies: as a *void* it signifies absence, the absence of Berlin's Jews, most of whom perished in the Holocaust.[13] As a *fractured* void it signifies history, a broken history without continuity: the history of Jews in Germany, of German Jews, and therefore also the history of Germany itself, which cannot be thought of as separate from Jewish history in Germany. Thus, in line with the original demand of the competition, the void provides that in-between space between Berlin's history and Jewish history in Berlin, inseparable as they are, except that it does it in a form radically different from what was originally imagined by the competition. By leaving this in-between space void, the museum's architecture forecloses the possibility of re-harmonizing German-Jewish history along the discredited models of symbiosis or assimilation. But it also forecloses the opposite view that sees the Holocaust as the inevitable telos of German history. Jewish life in Germany has been fundamentally altered by the Holocaust, but it has not stopped. The void thus becomes a space nurturing memory and reflection for Jews and for Germans. Its very presence points to an absence that can never be overcome, a rupture that cannot be healed, and that can certainly not be filled with museal stuff. Its fundamental epistemological negativity cannot be absorbed into the narratives that will be told by the objects and installations in the showrooms of the museum. The void will always be there in the minds of the spectators crossing the bridges that traverse it as they move through the exhibition space. The spectators themselves will move constantly between the lines. Organized around a void without images, Libeskind's architecture has become script. His building itself writes the discontinuous narrative that is Berlin, inscribes it physically into the very movement of the museum visitor, and yet opens a space for remembrance to be articulated and read between the lines.

Of course, the voids I have been juxtaposing in this essay are of a fundamentally different nature. One is an open urban space resulting from war, destruction, and a series of subsequent historical events; the other is an architectural space, consciously constructed and self-reflexive to the core. Both spaces nurture memory, but whose memory? The very notion of the void will have different meaning for Jews than it will for Germans. There is a danger of romanticizing or naturalizing the voided center of Berlin, just as Libeskind's building may ultimately not avoid the reproach of aestheticizing or monumentalizing the void architecturally.[14] But then the very articulation of this museal space demonstrates the architect's awareness of the dangers of monumentality: huge as the expansion is, the spectator can never see or experience it as a whole. Both the void inside and the building as perceived from the outside elude the totalizing gaze upon which monumental effects are predicated. Spatial monumentality is undercut in the inevitably temporal apprehension of the building. Such antimonumental monumentality, with which the museum memorializes both the Holocaust and Jewish life in Berlin, stands in sharp contrast to

FIGURE 3.10 Void inside the Jewish Museum. Courtesy Büro Daniel Libeskind.

the unself-conscious monumentality of the official government-sponsored Holocaust Monument, which is to be built at the northern end of that highly charged space between the Brandenburg Gate and Leipziger Platz.[15] For those who for good reasons question the ability of traditional monuments to keep memory alive as public or collective memory, Libeskind's expansion of the Berlin Museum may be a better memorial to German and Jewish history, the history of the living and of the dead, than any official funereal Holocaust monument could possibly be.[16]

As architecture, then, Libeskind's museum is the only project in the current Berlin building boom that explicitly articulates issues of national and local history in ways pertinent to post-unification Germany. In its spatial emphasis on the radical ruptures, discontinuities, and fractures of German and German-Jewish history, it stands in opposition to the critical reconstructionists' attempts to create a seamless continuity with a pre-1914 national past that would erase memories of Weimar, Nazi, and GDR architecture in the process. As an architecture of memory, it also opposes the postnationalism of global corporate architecture à la Potsdamer and Leipziger Platz, an architecture of development that has neither memory nor sense of place to begin with. As an unintentional manifesto, the museum points to the conceptual emptiness that currently exists between a nostalgic pre-1914 understanding of the city and its post-2002 entropic corporate malling. The history of Berlin as a void is not over yet, but then perhaps a city as vast and vibrant as Berlin will manage to incorporate its latest white elephants at Potsdamer and Leipziger Platz into the larger urban fabric. If Paris is able to live with Sacre Coeur, who is to say that Berlin cannot stomach Sony Corp.? Once the current image frenzy is over, the INFO BOX dismantled, and the critical reconstructionists forgotten, the notion of the capital as a montage of many historical forms and spaces will reassert itself, and the commitment to the necessarily palimpsestic texture of urban space may even lead to new, not yet imaginable forms of architecture.

4

After the War: Berlin as Palimpsest

I

When the German Reichstag, renovated and crowned with a stunning glass cupola by Sir Norman Foster, was inaugurated with a plenary session of parliament on April 19, 1999, the Berlin Republic was at war in Kosovo. A fact that could only have caused revulsion ten years ago now met with broad public approval. Two months later, and decades after the German Wehrmacht last moved through these rugged Balkan mountains, beating a retreat from southeastern Europe, German ground troops have moved into a southwestern swath of Kosovo as part of NATO's peace-keeping mission, and they are celebrated as liberators by the Kosovo Albanians. It is the cunning of history that all this should be happening under the stewardship of a social-democratic chancellor and a Green minister of foreign affairs, representatives of the very political forces that vociferously opposed NATO and the Gulf War in the early 1990s. But it indicates how much the Federal Republic of Germany has expanded its geographic and political horizons since unification in 1990.

Ten years after the fall of the Wall the Berlin Republic is part of a new constellation in Europe. No major antiwar demonstrations have rocked Berlin as they did during the Gulf War, when white bedsheets fluttered from Berlin balconies, pigs' blood was spilled by demonstrators in the streets in angry protest, and the country was caught up in convulsions of pacifism. At that time of mounting inner-German tensions, the East German and West German Left could revel in the common anti-American slogan "no blood for oil." The scene in all Germany then was in stark contrast to the public support the Gulf War enjoyed in London or Paris. Today, Germany is politically in sync with other NATO capitals, even though opposition to the Kosovo War is strong in East Berlin among the supporters of the revamped Communist Party, the PDS. But especially in the first month of the bombing campaign, the republic remained eerily quiet, and commentators marveled at the surprising change of heart that seemed to have overcome German public opinion, which used to be quite adamant in its principled antiwar stance.

But is that really what it is—a change of heart? Sure, the decision to join the war effort was now made by a social democratic–Green coalition government bedeviled by a rocky start in domestic politics and badly in need of political success. And though some called Schröder the "war chancellor," many on the Left and among the Greens grudgingly kept up their support for the new government. But underlying the acceptance of Germany's role in the Kosovo conflict was something else. The two meanings of Germany's categorical imperative "never again" have come into irreconcilable conflict with each other over Slobodan Milosevic's persistent policies of ethnic cleansing. The "never again" of deploying German troops in an "out-of-area" mission not geared toward purely defensive goals stands against the "never again" that recognizes German responsibility for the Holocaust, emphatically requiring action at the advent of any crisis even remotely reminiscent of the Holocaust. The antimilitary imperative not to deploy German troops out-of-area thus clashed with the moral imperative to intervene in the Balkan genocide. If the politics of memory have dominated the German consensus of "never again," then it was precisely memories of World War II that whittled away at the understandable reluctance to use German troops out-of-area: television images of endless streams of refugees fleeing ethnic cleansing, women and children packed into trains for deportation, stories of mass executions, rape, looting, and wanton destruction.

Of course, it is not entirely clear what Germans remembered. Was it the refugees from Nazism and the victims of German occupation? Or did viewers have Germans in mind, Germans as refugees from the Red Army, expellees from Silesia and from Czechoslovakia? Or was it both rolled into one, the problematic universalism of victimhood? Whatever the case may be, the strength of memory legitimized the intervention for the vast majority of Germans, even at the price of having to betray one of their two most dearly held convictions. For many, it was a painful choice to make and a blow to the self-righteousness that had accrued to the joint litany of "no more war" and "no more Auschwitz" over the years.

As the bombing campaign failed to produce instant success, voices of protest arose and became increasingly vociferous. They were fed by the old anti-Americanism of the Left and by a new, equally anti-American Euronationalism on the Right, but contrary to the Gulf War, they lacked broad public resonance. Nevertheless, NATO's blunders breathed new life into the "no more war" position. Not surprisingly, one fault line divided the resolutely antiwar stance of the PDS from the pro-NATO position of the other parties, a replay of the continuing East-West divide within Germany. But a rift also appeared not just *among* intellectuals, who after all had been divided about the Gulf War as well (Hans Magnus Enzensberger and Biermann against the antiwar Left in 1991), but between antiwar intellectuals such as Peter Handke and Klaus Theweleit on the one hand and publicly supported government policy on the other. The difference is that in 1991 the pro-intervention literati broke with the national antiwar consensus, while this time the opposition to intervention remained the minority voice. Even as there are good reasons to be skeptical in principle about a military human rights intervention and critical of long-term Western policy in the Balkans, insisting on the principle of national sovereignty in the face of Milosevic's serial wars of ethnic cleansing had to appear outright cynical. A new politics of memory and historical trauma has emerged at the core of transatlantic culture in the past ten years, and in the case of Kosovo, it won the strong yet uneasy support of the public despite serious doubts about the universal applicability of human rights intervention in the affairs of sovereign states. But this was Europe, the continent where the Holocaust had taken place. Europe would have lost all political legitimacy in its drive toward unification had it allowed the Serbian genocide to continue. Here, the German politics of memory and the politics of the new Europe merged. The political change is stunning.

The Kosovo War has shaken up German politics, and it will have an impact on the new Europe. At a minimum, the Balkans and its Muslims have now been recognized as a constitutive part of a unified Europe. Ten years after the fall of the Wall, which was greeted at the time with a mix of genuine triumph and subliminal fears of a resurgent German nationalism, the emerging Berlin Republic is a European republic and Berlin a European capital among others. And the new Berlin, the new reunited Germany is new in ways hardly imagined ten years ago when the triumphalists of national sovereignty dreamed about a self-confident nation (*selbstbewußte Nation*) that would finally overcome its past, while the detractors of national unification painted the horror vision of a Fourth Reich. Today, Germany is neither. Two weeks after German troops moved into Kosovo, the German parliament affirmed the Berlin Republic's commitment to commemorate the Holocaust. The much-debated though still controversial Memorial to the Murdered Jews of Europe will be built in the very heart of Berlin. Only time will tell whether this memorial will nurture commemoration or foster oblivion, but the decision to go ahead with the project is politically significant, even though the decision itself was reached with a sense of exhaustion after a twelve-year-long debate.

II

If memories of the past and an evolving present have mixed in unforeseeable ways in the politics of the Berlin Republic, then the same can be said about the architectural reconstruction of Berlin as Germany's capital. At a time when many building projects are coming to fruition, the assessment of the new Berlin has become more fluid and ambiguous than it was five years ago. The stifling architectural debate then pitted the traditionalists of "critical reconstruction" against the triumphalists of postmodern high tech, and both faced the radical skeptics who diagnosed a total lack of any persuasive urban or architectural vision on either side of that debate. Today the boundaries that separated the various factions seem blurred. Critical reconstruction with its restrictive regulations and its ideology of building in stone has never become as dominant a Procrustean bed for the new Berlin architecture as some had feared. Some high-tech projects have been absorbed rather well into the city fabric. And even though there may still not be anything resembling a cohesive urban vision, a decentered network of new building sites and changing neighborhoods is emerging that is increasingly being accepted by the public and that has begun to shape the image of Berlin as a partly creative, partly timid mix of old and new.

The rebuilt Reichstag may serve as an emblem for this mix of the cre-

FIGURE 4.1 Reichstag under renovation. Architect: Norman Foster (1998).
Photo: author.

ative and the timid at this time. Its facade and shell are the only residues
left from Wilhelmian times: up to three-meter-deep stone walls, pompous
columns, a lot of monumental stone permeated by historical reminiscences. The inside of the building has been totally ripped out and prag-
matically, though coldly, refurbished in muted materials and colors, but
the graffiti left by Soviet soldiers in 1945 are still visible and highlighted on
several walls. The only real architectural attraction is the Reichstag's
cupola, destroyed by arson in the first year of Nazi rule and redesigned by
Norman Forster as a gigantic glass dome, oddly reminiscent of a beehive
or an oversize space egg.

The double winding ramps on the inside are publicly accessible, providing panoramic views of the surrounding city and setting the open inte-
rior spaces of the building into slow motion for the walking spectator, a
veritable "flaneur dans l'air." But it is especially the illuminated dome at
night that has been embraced by the media and the public as a symbol of
the new Berlin. Foster's overall renovation may not satisfy on purely aesthetic grounds, but it successfully embodies the tensions between the

FIGURE 4.2 Reichstag cupola, outside view. Architect: Norman Foster (1999). Photo: author.

unloved imperial past (the building's outside shell), a bureaucratic functional present of the German republic (the plenary hall for the Bundestag), and the desire to have a flashy image of democratic transparency marking Berlin's reclaimed status as capital.

At times in the early 1990s, it seemed that the old would overwhelm any new departure. The consensus was that Berlin was primarily a memory space, haunted by the ghosts of its past: Berlin as the center of a discontinuous, ruptured history, site of the collapse of four successive German states, command center of the Holocaust, capital of German communism in the Cold War, and flash point of the East-West confrontation of the nuclear age. Obsessed with its memories as they were stirred up after the fall of the Wall, the city simultaneously plunged into a frenzy of urban planning and architectural megaprojects that were to codify the new beginning and to guarantee Berlin's metropolitan image for decades to come. Ghosts of the past and the spirit of future glory struggled on the same terrain without prospects for reconciliation. With the emergence of major new building plans in the historical center of Berlin for the

FIGURE 4.3 Reichstag cupola, inside view. Photo: author.

government quarter and the Reichstag, the corporate center at Leipziger and Potsdamer Platz, the restoration of Pariser Platz, the emerging plans for the Museumsinsel, Alexanderplatz, and for the preservation of the Stalinist urbanism of the Karl-Marx-Allee (formerly Stalinallee, now Frankfurter Allee), presence and absence, memory and forgetting entered into a fascinating mix. Heated conflict erupted even over the marginalia of urban reorganization. Communist monuments in East Berlin were knocked down and street names were changed, triggering a public debate about the legacies of the socialist state and the politics of forgetting. Some wanted to raze the East German Palace of the Republic, plagued by asbestos but quite popular among East Berliners, and in its stead rebuild the Hohenzollern Palace, which was bombed out in World War II and razed by the communists in the 1950s. Talk about the voids of Berlin became commonplace. The vast empty space in Berlin Mitte between the Brandenburg Gate in the north and the Potsdamer Platz in the south, which had been occupied by the mine strip and the Wall, now cleared away, captured the imagination. Visibility and invisibility became categories of architectural discourse about the built legacies of the fascist and communist states. Which buildings should be given over to the wrecking ball and which should be reutilized once the government moved from Bonn to Berlin? Even the unbuilt past, Albert Speer's megalomaniac plans for the triumphal north-south axis and the transformation of Berlin into Germania as capital of the Third Reich, exerted its power over any visions of the future. Thus the plans for the new government strip in the bend of the Spree River just north of the Reichstag studiously avoided a north-south layout, opting instead for an east-west axis that had the additional advantage of suggesting reconciliation between the two parts of the city separated from each other for so long by the Cold War. But then Christo's wrapping of the Reichstag in 1995 provided a stunning reprieve from the burden of dark memories. The dialectic of the visible and the invisible found its exuberant and celebratory expression in this temporary installation that charmed Berliners and the world and that now finds its counterpoint in Norman Foster's radiant glass dome.

But visibility and invisibility, memory and forgetting have yet another dimension in the debate about reconstructing the German capital. At stake is the question of the center, of the centered city. Many saw the void left by the dismantled Wall in Berlin's middle as a scar that might never heal, either architecturally or historically. Historically, of course, this space never was a center. Instead it marked the boundary between the old Berlin, east of the Brandenburg Gate, and its western expansion through the Tiergarten district and beyond. Even the Reichstag, built as the imperial parliament in the 1890s, was banned from the inner sanctum of imperial Berlin, which began only east of the Brandenburg Gate. Architecturally, any radically new vision for this space left by the vanished Wall was quickly blocked by the political logic of developing the new government strip in the Spreebogen and by the hasty approval of the corporate development plans at Potsdamer and Leipziger Platz. The empty space in the center thus has shrunk, but it still suggests a void, something that remains unsaid in the urban text.

In a certain way, this void right on top of Speer's north-south axis conjures up the void that cuts through the famous zigzag structure of Daniel Libeskind's Jewish Museum. Libeskind's void is an architectural index of the destruction of Berlin's Jews and their rich culture during the Third Reich. The void between Brandenburg Gate and Potsdamer Platz, on the other hand, between the government mall and the corporate headquarters, may in the end not signify the loss of a potential new urban center that was not to be. It rather suggests that Berlin cannot be centered in the same way that London or Paris are.

The defining power of this symbolic space in the heart of Berlin is only exacerbated by the fact that it is precisely in this void, just south of the Brandenburg Gate and very close to where Hitler's Reichskanzlei once stood, that the Berlin Republic is to build the Memorial to the Murdered Jews of Europe. After twelve years of public controversy, multiple competitions, changing juries, political denunciations, and a radical about-face of several of the participants in the debate about the politics, aesthetics, and purpose of such a monument, the memorial, designed by Peter Eisenman as a labyrinthine field of some 2,500 stone slabs of differing height and complemented by a documentation center, will finally be erected. The parliamentary debate was uninspired, but a political decision was needed to legitimize the project democratically and to put an end to public wrangling. Everybody recognizes that there can be no perfect solution to memorializing the Holocaust in the country of its perpetrators. But it must be commemorated, through an act of political will and with a commitment to the democratic future, even though any monument will always run the risk of becoming just another testimony to forgetting, a cipher of invisibility. Thus in the very center of the new Berlin, there will be a national memorial to German crimes against humanity, that ultimate rupture of Western civilization which has come to be seen by some as emblematic of the twentieth century as a whole, a curse on the house of modernity that we now inhabit with enormous trepidation.

III

Talk of the voids of Berlin, however, seems less pertinent now than it was a few years ago. Indeed, the urban tabula rasa fantasies of the early 1990s have faded fast. Enthusiasm about building the new Berlin from scratch is giving way to a more pragmatic outlook. Not metaphors of the void but emptiness is the issue at a time when so many new office and apartment buildings are still looking for occupants. At the federal level, financial calculations have forced a scaling back of many plans, mandating reutilization rather than destruction of several major fascist buildings in the heart of Berlin (Göring's aviation ministry and the Reichsbank). Overblown images of a new global Berlin as capital of the twenty-first century have made way for a more modest reality. What is now emerging is the more intriguing notion of Berlin as palimpsest, a disparate city-text that is being rewritten while previous text is preserved, traces are restored, erasures documented, all of it resulting in a complex web of historical markers that point to the continuing heterogeneous life of a vital city that is as ambivalent of its built past as it is of its urban future.

Berlin is now past the point when the debate focused primarily on the vast corporate construction site at Potsdamer and Leipziger Platz. Gigantic developments by Daimler Benz and Sony loomed large as threats to the urban fabric as a whole. The malling of Potsdamer Platz, that mythic traffic hub of the Weimar Republic, Germany's Piccadilly Circus and Times Square rolled into one, seemed a foregone conclusion and a symbol of all bad things to come. Potsdamer Platz has indeed been malled, and the architectural results are, as predicted, rather appalling. Its relationship to the neighboring Kulturforum with the Staatsbibliothek, the Philharmonie (both by Hans Scharoun) and the Neue Nationalgalerie (Mies van der Rohe) is ill defined. The new Potsdamer Platz will never match the myth of the square as an emblem of Weimar modernity. The narrative of Pots-

FIGURE 4.4 The new Potsdamer Platz plaza. Photo: author.

damer Platz as the imaginary center of a metropolis expires in its arcades, which, as a two-story drab shopping mall stuffed with mini-boutiques and fast-food units, resembles the inside of a prison more closely than a consumer paradise.

   And yet, Potsdamer Platz in its new incarnation has received a surprisingly positive press, and the public seems to accept it with open arms. To some, the city's insistence on maintaining the old street plans for the Potsdamer Platz area has turned out to be a blessing in disguise. For the narrow streets, alleys, and piazzas allow for a certain intensity of street life, as long as one forgets that it is the street life of the late twentieth century: that of the pedestrian shopping mall. Others feel that the corporate and commercial buildings are different enough in size, material, and design at least to suggest a real urban space. If it is a mall, to them it is also still Potsdamer Platz. Much will depend on how these buildings age and how attractive Potsdamer Platz will remain as a public space once its current novelty has worn off. I remain skeptical, but Potsdamer Platz today may well embody the structural irreconcilability between consumer society and public space.

   At any rate, the Potsdamer Platz development, the white elephant of

Berlin reconstruction, has been joined by other architectural attractions. There now is a web of sites of very different size and function that fleshes out the architectural landscape of the new Berlin: the new Pariser Platz just east of the Brandenburg Gate, an entryway into classical Berlin; the Hackesche Höfe, an imaginative reutilization of one of the most fabled multiple inner courtyards of the old Berlin; the Aldo Rossi complex of apartment buildings and offices at Schützenstraße, with its southern-style courtyards and colorful and varied facades that loosen up the block building prescriptions of critical reconstruction; the fast-paced renovations at Prenzlauer Berg, in the old Jewish quarter known as Scheunenviertel, and in other neighborhoods of East Berlin. In fact, East Berlin is architecturally at an advantage. Since the poverty of the East German state prevented wholesale destruction of old housing stock, the preservation and restoration of neighborhoods is now possible in a way forever barred to most of the western parts of the city. The political conflicts between East and West Berliners, however, linger on. They have even intensified as the new city is slowly taking shape and as parts of East Berlin are being gentrified. But then, in one way or another, the eastern part of Berlin was always separated from its western part, and the current "wall in the head" may just be the latest manifestation of a long tradition. Architecturally neglected in most discussions are of course those socialist mass housing projects (Plattenbau) in East Berlin known from all over Eastern Europe. And yet it would be quite challenging to imagine ways of integrating housing projects such as Marzahn, Hohenschönhausen, and especially Hellersdorf into the new urban fabric, now that they have lost their grounding in socialist notions of collective living. Whether they will stand as ruins of socialism and urban decay or whether they can be modified in some creative form, only time will tell. The larger question here is to what extent the socialist city text will remain part of the fast-changing palimpsest that is Berlin. Daniel Libeskind's plan for Alexanderplatz pointed creatively in that direction, but it has no chance of being realized.

IV

A mix of the old and the new, the creative and the timid—that does not seem all that bad a constellation for a city that has never had the luster of London or the aura of Paris. Building on its historical decenteredness as an architectural urban space and maintaining the city as a palimpsest of many different times and histories may actually be preferable to the notion of a centered Berlin that would inevitably revive the ghosts of the past, not just in the minds of Germans but in the imagination of Germany's neighbors east and west. Berlin as palimpsest implies voids, illegibilities, and erasures, but it also offers a richness of traces and memories, restorations and new contructions that will mark the city as lived space. Bernhard Schlink, author of the best-selling novel *The Reader*, is certainly right in suggesting that Berlin still lacks a physical and psychological center. I see this as an advantage, and in that sense the title for the architectural sight-seeing tours, organized by the city in the summers of the late 1990s, may not be inappropriate after all: *Berlin—offene Stadt*, Berlin—open city.

5

Fear of Mice: The Times Square Redevelopment

I

Cats, the longest-running show on Broadway, was approaching its twentieth year at the Winter Garden, just a few blocks north of Times Square, in the late 1990s, but the fear of a mouse had become the dominant trope in the debate about the Times Square redevelopment. Listening to some critics wax apocalyptic about the effects of Disney's invasion into the inner sanctum of New York city's popular culture reminds me of how much the Nazis hated Mickey as a symbol of the pollution of authentic German culture. To the Nazis, the mouse was dark, filthy, a carrier of disease, a threat to the body politic and to the body of the nation.[1] Within Germany of the 1930s, of course, the mouse was the Jew. In the 1940 propaganda film *The Eternal Jew*, the Jewish diaspora is represented as swarms of migrating rodents invading, destroying, and controlling every part of the globe. It was a theory of globalization *avant la lettre*: intensely paranoid, conspiratorial, and murderously ideological. Reacting to the success of Disney movies in Germany, the Nazis focused on Mickey's blackness, warned of the "negroidization" (*Verniggerung*) of German culture, and thus conflated Disney with their attack on jazz as that other mode of American, i.e., un-German, culture that needed to be excised: Louis Armstrong and Benny Goodman—this black-Jewish combination represented the ultimate overdetermined cultural threat to the Aryan race. Given their phobia about mice, the Nazis were unable to see how well Disney fit into their own ideological project: cleanliness, anti-urbanism, chauvinism, xenophobia combined with a privileging of grand spectacle and mass entertainment as it was organized by Goebbels's ministry of illusion.[2] The Aryan beauty could have come to love the little American beast, but the match between Disney and Nazi Germany never came to pass.

The Nazis had their own version of Disneyworld, a world without mice, to be sure, based on deadly serious monumentalism rather than on comics, but also predicated on control, spectacle, simulacrum, and megalomania. In architecture, it was Albert Speer's Germania, the new capital of the Thousand-Year Reich, designed in the late 1930s and scheduled to be built by 1950. Well, American and British bombers cleared the ground for Germania's north-south axis in the center of Berlin, but in such a way as to guarantee that it would never be built. Instead, Germany, like everybody else in Cold War Europe, got Disney. And jazz, and blues, and rock 'n' roll. To German teenagers in the 1950s all these American cultural imports—only later decried as American cultural imperialism—were a breath of fresh air. They opened a window to the world enabling a whole generation to define itself untraditionally in the midst of the rubble and ruins left from the Third Reich. Even reading Mickey Mouse and Donald Duck could count as an act of resistance to that "authentic" German popular culture that had survived the Third Reich, was force-fed in the schools in *Volkslied* choirs, and dominated the film industry in the form of the *Heimatfilm*. Disney and its effects—it's a complicated story, not easily reducible to a homogeneous plot.

II

Of course, the comparison between today's Disney critics and the Nazis is unfair. Another time, another politics, true enough. And yet, how well the Nazi image of the mouse fits a certain Times Square imaginary, not that of the Square of today, but that of a time *before* the current redevelopment: sex shops, sleaze, drugs, prostitution, child abuse, urban decay. Forty-second Street embodied it all. Ever since, we've had the irreconcilable antagonism between the ideological cleanup crews of the Right and the romantics of marginality on the Left. But as in the case of the Nazis, a mythic image of a better past is conjured up in either case to fend off change. Throughout history this trope of nostalgia has proven to be as singularly attractive as it has been elusive in the long run, for it is unable to anchor its mythic notion of authenticity in the real world. Authenticity, it seems, always comes after, and then primarily as loss. In city culture particularly, the resisted new is bound to become the basis for another glorified past some time in the future. Therefore, it seems preferable to side with Bertolt Brecht against the good old days and in favor of the bad new ones. For it was not evident at all that the mere presence of Disney in Times Square with a store and a theater would transform that whole space into another Disneyland. New York, after all, ain't Anaheim, and the recent transformation of Times Square involves much more than just the presence of entertainment conglomerates such as Disney, Bertelsmann, and Viacom. In its current incarnation, at any rate, Times Square seems a lot more attractive than what was being planned a mere ten years ago. Have we forgotten Philip Johnson and John Burgee's office towers, which charitably went on hold after the 1987 financial crash? Rather than turning Times Square into an office wasteland populated by gray guys in three-piece suits, the recent redevelopment directed by Robert Stern acknowledges the space as a center of theaters, entertainment, and advertising culture. That is something to build on. It is almost already traditional.

III

This is not to embrace Disney as panacea, and Disney's presence in Times Square may indeed be an indication of urban developments that are not altogether salutary. But we should speak of them in a different key. The reaction, at any rate, should not be a flight toward some notion of a residual or uncontaminated higher culture, a position from which one would then go on to lament the relentless commercialization of culture invoked with the Disney name. The Times Square redevelopment is symptomatic of a reorientation of the axes of cultural debate. The fissures are no longer between high and low, elite and commercial culture, as they were in the postmodernism debate of the 1970s and 1980s, but they crack open in the very realm of the "popular" itself. Even the 1930s debate between Adorno and Benjamin on mass culture, which has become a standard reference point for all those populist critics who simply turn the old hierarchy on its head, cannot be reduced to the simplistic dichotomy of high vs. low.

Early on, Adorno did understand the insidiously reactionary side of Disney's project, locating it in what he heard as the sadomasochistic glee of audiences laughing their heads off every time the little guy gets punished or is beaten up: the Donald Duck syndrome, mass culture as mass deception and collective sadomasochism.[3] Adorno's condemnation of Mickey Mouse was as total as that of the Nazis, but for reasons that had to do with class rather than race. Walter Benjamin famously disagreed with Adorno's assessment, basing his more positive take on Mickey on his insights into how modern media may radically alter modes of perception of the world, how they can explode fixed perceptions of time and space, how the cartoon mouse on celluloid might even represent some dreamed-of reconciliation between modern technical media and nature. The issue even then was not merely high vs. low, but rather how to evaluate forms of a commercial mass culture that were transported and shaped by new media. This is still the issue today. In the debate about Times Square we have the sparring of two different concepts of mass culture and of the popular: one that is clean, mainstream, suburban, and focused on family values, the other invariably identifying the truly popular with notions of marginality, sexual politics, otherness, and minority culture. Both views are narrow, and it is not at all clear why Times Square should exclusively belong to either one.

At any rate, the question of high vs. low that obsessed the postmodernism debate is simply not relevant for a discussion of Times Square today. It would be too easy to accuse the prophets of Disneydoomsday of secretly harboring intellectual and high-cultural prejudices against the pleasures of mass culture. Some of their arguments against the Disney empire, after all, are absolutely on target and not linked to the high/low opposition. In fact, their ideological critique of the Disney vision of a global mass culture could be lifted right out of Adorno, an "elitist" theorist with whom today's American critics of Disney would refuse to have any traffic.

IV

What is at stake with Times Square, in my view, is the transformation of a fabled place of popular culture in an age in which global entertainment conglomerates are rediscovering the value of the city and its millions of tourists for their marketing strategies.[4] The Times Square redevelopment project pits those who lament the loss of an older, somehow authentic Times Square—whether in its allegedly healthy incarnation of the 1940s or the grimy, X-rated, and decayed one of more recent vintage—against those who are open to change but not sure yet what the change will entail in terms of economics, traffic, ambiance, and vibrancy in this symbolic center of Manhattan. Surely, there will be some mall-like environments in the new Times Square, and there will be more theme parking in restaurants and shops, but you can't even blame all of that on Disney. The mall has invaded the urban centers and it is here to stay. Just walk into the Marriott Marquis (built in the Reagan era as a fortress against Forty-second Street sleaze) and you will find New Jersey in Manhattan—a wholly suburbanized urban space, complete with predictable greenery, mallish escalators and inside/outside high-speed elevators. Like a vertical Garden State Parkway, these glass elevators racing silently up and down transport you quickly to your destination in the vertical grid. At the same time this vertical suburbia offers one of the most stunning views available onto an urban scene: from the eighth-floor revolving bar one can see the panorama of Times Square, the flashing billboards, the teeming crowds down below in the canyon, the streams of cars and taxis, the city as artificial paradise of color, movement, and light. This view by itself is proof that the real suburbia no longer satisfies its inhabitants, who are flocking back to the city as tourists and consumers in search of entertainment and spectacle.

This is also where the larger problem emerges. It is what I would describe as the city as image. It is a problem New York shares with other major nineteenth- and twentieth-century cities struggling to maintain their role as centers of business and commerce while at the same time transforming themselves into museal environments for an increasingly globalized cultural tourism. The discourse of the city as image is one of urban politicians and developers trying to guarantee revenue from mass tourism, from conventions, and from commercial and office rental. Central to this new kind of urban politics are aesthetic spaces for cultural consumption, blockbuster museal events, and spectacles of many kinds, all intended to lure that new species of the city tourist, the urban vacationer, who has replaced the older, leisurely flaneur who was always figured as a dweller rather than as a traveler from afar. Surely, there is a downside to this notion of the city as image, as museum or theme park. But one need only compare the current Times Square developments to the Sony and Daimler developments of Berlin's Potsdamer Platz to lay such worries at least

FIGURE 5.1 Current construction at southwest corner of Forty-second Street and Seventh Ave. Site of the former Disney store (2001). Photo: author.

partly to rest.[5] The famous hub between the east and west of Berlin is in great danger of becoming a high-tech mall. The new Potsdamer Platz is being built on a site that has been, for fifty years, a wasteland, first destroyed in World War II and then cut through by the Wall. Times Square, on the other hand, has not lost its urban energy and vibrancy, nor is it likely to do so in the future. More tourists, yes, but then perhaps also growing theater audiences again and all the subsidiary economies that might revitalize the area.

None of this, however, requires us to celebrate the new Times Square as an art installation, the ultimate incarnation of a commercial billboard culture that has now become indistinguishable from real art, as an article in the *New York Times* recently suggested a bit too triumphantly.[6] Earlier in this century, the Austrian language critic Karl Kraus had a point when he insisted that there is a difference between an urn and a chamber pot, and divided his contemporaries into those who use the chamber pot as an urn and those who use the urn as a chamber pot. But if it is now common practice to do both at once, which seems the case in much postmodern culture, then perhaps we should reconsider such distinctions. Distinctions are important to make when discussing the transformations of urban space brought on by the new service and entertainment economies. There are good reasons to believe that Times Square will remain a site of urban diversity rather than become a mere colony in the Disney empire. Let's not forget that Disney's lease at the corner of Forty-second Street and Seventh Avenue is temporary. Disney's New York experiment may yet fail, and the office towers may still be built.[7] Which might even make a Disney Times Square into an object of nostalgia . . .

Coda

September 2001. More than four years after this text was first presented at a symposium on Times Square at Columbia University's Graduate School of Architecture, Planning and Preservation, Times Square has still not found its final new form. Three corporate towers at the corners of Forty-second Street and Seventh Avenue were built after all during the boom of the late 1990s, and the fourth one is currently under construction.

As a result, the much maligned Disney store, across Forty-second Street from the New Victory Theater renovated by Disney, has disappeared,

FIGURE 5.2 New Victory Theater. Across from former Disney store on Forty-second Street. Photo: author.

and the Disney paranoia of a few years ago now seems even more overblown. It is yet another irony that the conservative attempt of the 1990s to rid Manhattan of its sex industry to "ready Times Square for Snow White" has only resulted in redirecting the pornography trade to unlikely places like the Hasidic-run diamond district and even to the area around Gracie Mansion, residence of "quality of life" mayor Rudolph Giuliani.[8]

There are good reasons to think that Disney was never a good match with real urban space. But the real threat to a lived metropolitan urbanity, as we now know, emanates from entirely other quarters. The events of September 11 will divide the history of this city—and not just of this city—into a before and an after. Not only has the skyline of southern Manhattan been changed forever, but so has the domestic and global imaginary of New York as a whole.

I never quite understood why some loved the old seedy Times Square so much. But I do understand how the architecturally plain if not ugly twin towers of the World Trade Center, which had been strongly opposed by most New Yorkers at the planning stage, could for so many become an emblem of New York—a marker of home for the city's inhabitants, a powerful image of late-twentieth-century America for international tourists and business, and an icon for both the benefits and the downside of globalization. Their collapse has left a gaping hole in our vision of the city, like a retinal disintegration in the imagination. Already there are voices suggesting that Times Square be turned into a mall to protect it from car bombs. But turning public urban space into a new kind of gated neighborhood would mean that the terrorists have already won. At any rate, the predictions after September 11 that the era of the skyscraper has ended is now being challenged by the re-redevelopment of the four corners of Forty-second Street and Seventh Avenue. Now, as through much of the 1990s, Times Square is a construction site. No more than Disney's arrival in New York heralded the end of metropolitan culture will the bombing of the twin towers close the chapter on the architecture of tall buildings.

Memory Sites in an Expanded Field: The Memory Park in Buenos Aires

I

Struggles over public memory involving historical trauma, genocide, human rights violations, and their aftereffects abound in the world today. Monuments, memorials, public sculptures, commemorative sites, and museums are being created at an accelerated pace the world over. The power of such sites to support public memory narratives rather than simply to freeze the past is very much at issue everywhere, and there are no easy solutions to be had.

Memory politics is writ large at the national and international levels, not just in the United States and Europe, but in East Asia, Australia, South Africa, and Latin America. In one way or another, issues of memory no longer simply concern the past but have become part of the very political legitimacy of regimes today, and they shape the ethical self-understanding of societies vis-à-vis their conflictual history and the world. If, in the earlier twentieth century, modern societies tried to define their modernity and to secure their cohesiveness by way of imagining the future, it now seems that the major required task of any society today is to take responsibility for its past. Whether this kind of memory work will result in some new code of international ethics remains questionable, but it does indicate something about our present that points beyond the cynicism of enlightened false consciousness and mere Realpolitik.

Print and image media contribute liberally to the vertiginous swirl of memory discourses that circulate globally and locally. We read about Chinese and Korean comfort women and the rape of Nanjing; we hear about the "stolen generation" in Australia and the killing and kidnapping of children during the dirty war in Argentina; we read about Truth and Reconciliation Commissions in South Africa and Guatemala; and we have become witnesses to an ever-growing number of public apologies by politicians for misdeeds of the past. Certainly, the voraciousness of the media and their appetite for recycling seems to be the sine qua non of local memory discourses crossing borders, entering into a network of cross-national comparisons, and creating what one might call a global culture of memory.

Some historians have expressed their discomfort with the surfeit of memory in contemporary culture, raising serious questions about the depth and the effects of our obsessions with memory. Others very explicitly lament what they see as the present being held hostage to the past. After all, the desire to forget always seems to grow in proportion to the desire to remember, especially when problematic aspects of a nation's past are at stake. Memory and amnesia always exist side by side and remain part of a political struggle. But the debate about the surfeit or even excess of memory in contemporary culture ignores one important factor: especially since 1989 and in societies that find themselves in a complex process of transition (South Africa, Latin American countries, China), discussions about how to remember the past have morphed into an international debate about human rights, restitution, and justice, replete with NGOs (nongovernmental organizations), extradition requests, and prosecution across borders. This debate depends on the recognition of specific pasts as much as it is really concerned with the future. My hypothesis here is that human rights activism in the world today depends very much on the depth and breadth of memory discourses in the public media.

And then there is something else to consider. However different the mode or medium of commemorating may be in each local or regional case, all such struggles about how to remember a traumatic past of genocide, racial oppression, and dictatorship play themselves out in the much larger and more encompassing memory culture of this turn of the century in which national patrimony and heritage industries thrive, nostalgias of all kinds abound, and mythic pasts are being resurrected or created. Memory politics, indeed, seems as much a global project as it is always locally or nationally inflected. Memory projects may construct or revise national narratives (South Africa, Argentina, China), but these narratives are now invariably located in a space somewhere between the global and the local. This in-between space needs to be studied in its own right. The memory park in Buenos Aires I want to discuss here is a case in point for a story currently unfolding in Argentina, but being marked by what I would call in shorthand a traveling cross-national memory discourse.

II

Two brief words about my notion of the expanded field and its methodological implications. Memory sites have been discussed in terms of monuments and countermonuments, memorials and museums, transitory interventions in urban space, public art, and even marked sites in a landscape. My title is of course meant to be reminiscent of Rosalind Krauss's structuralist reading of "Sculpture in the Expanded Field."[1] That well-known essay of 1979 was an ambitious attempt to create a theoretical map for some of the most challenging sculptural practices of the 1960s and early 1970s. While my observations on the memory park project in Buenos Aires and its formal and aesthetic dimensions will like Krauss's essay be concerned with the relationship among sculpture, architecture, and landscape, I do have something different in mind with the notion of the expanded field. The expanded field here not only refers to the art-historical terms structuring Krauss's model. It also refers to political history (both in its implicit tracings and in its explicit articulation), and thus to temporality and memory, neither of which was central to Krauss's work at that time, which was concerned with the logic of sculptural form.

Second, I would also like to expand on Pierre Nora's notion of *lieux de mémoire*, translated as "realms of memory" in the American version.[2] Certainly, Nora's *lieux* do have a temporal and historical dimension. For the *lieux de mémoire* emerge only once collective memory has lost its power. Thus Nora's approach conveys a romantic sense of loss and melancholy that I find counterproductive in the case I am concerned with. For him, the *lieux de mémoire* come into being only after the *milieux de mémoire* that energized an earlier social and cultural formation have vanished, just as the retreating sea at low tide leaves isolated shells and rocks on the sandy bottoms, a problematic natural metaphor that Nora actually shares with Halbwachs's classical work on collective memory. More important—and this is the second point of my variance from Nora's otherwise very suggestive work—his project of mnemohistory is fundamentally tied to the idea of national memory, whereas I am precisely interested in the ways in which global dimensions intersect with the national or the local in the construction of memory sites in the contemporary world. The expanded field I am trying to construct thus involves the crossing of borders not only with regard to artistic medium (Krauss), but also in relation to geographies, politics, and the discourses of traumatic memory themselves (Nora). In this way, the *lieux de mémoire* today function not just in an expanded field but in a field altered by globalization.

III

So let me briefly introduce El Parque de la Memoria in Buenos Aires, for which ground was broken in early 2001. The project for this park emerged in Argentina out of the intense and long-standing political struggle about the fate of the *desaparecidos,* the thirty thousand or so who disappeared before and during the military dictatorship of the years 1976 to 1983. Ever since 1977, the public protests and weekly demonstrations of the Mothers and Grandmothers of the Plaza de Mayo in Buenos Aires have kept the terror of the Argentinean state against its own population in the public eye. International coverage of these protests, beginning with the soccer world championship of 1978, has provided a kind of security blanket at least for some of the protesters during the years of the dictatorship itself. Neither direct threats nor vilifications of the mothers as the madwomen of the Plaza de Mayo (*Las locas*) were able to distract this group of courageous women from their goal of establishing what happened to the disappeared, who was responsible for their incarceration and death, and who should stand trial for basic human rights violations.

When civilian rule was reestablished after Argentina's war against Britain over the Malvinas had gone awry, investigative commissions, documentations, retroactive laws, and amnesties under presidents Alfonsin and Menem in the late 1980s and early 1990s attempted to absolve Argentinean society from its responsibility for the state terror. But neither the 1986 law that became known as the *punto final* (Full Stop Law) for initiating new prosecutions, nor the 1987 law of *obediencia debida* or Law of Due

Obedience, nor even the general amnesty of 1990 that Menem granted to the members of the various juntas tried in 1985 was able to stop the mothers from seeking justice through the courts. For rape, theft, and the falsification of civil status of the kidnapped children of the disappeared were not covered under any of these attempts to achieve what Menem called reconciliation. Thus the patient and persistent work of the mothers and grandmothers to find the missing children with the help of genetic databanks has forced the country to keep facing the reality of state terror, and this attempt was helped in 1995 by a series of spectacular confessions by military men regarding their own participation in kidnappings, torture, and murder. Thus neither the legal conflict regarding how and whom to prosecute nor the cultural and political conflict of how to commemorate has ever died down. It has even intensified in recent years. Thus while there have been many events over the years such as performances and public demonstrations commemorating the disappeared, oral histories, testimonies, and the internationally acclaimed film *The Official Story*, the park project, sponsored by the city of Buenos Aires, is one of the first major instances in which public memory of the terror is given permanent shape in an urban setting in Argentina.

At the same time, there is a global dimension to the local controversy about the past. It is the discourse about the Holocaust and about Holocaust representations and memory that haunts or shadows the Argentinean debate. The point is not to compare the Holocaust to the Argentinean state terror against leftist "subversion," a politics born from the pathology of the Cold War combined with an ideology of purity and cleansing of the national body that Marguerite Feitlowitz has recently described in persuasive detail in her book *A Lexicon of Terror*.[3] In this context, one is of course reminded of the long history of anti-Semitism among the Argentinean elites; one could mention here that Argentina served as haven for Nazis like Eichmann and Mengele; or one could point to the disproportionately high number of Argentinean Jews among the disappeared. But the relationship to Holocaust discourse is not by way of comparison of the military dictatorship with Nazi Germany. It is rather by productive inscription of certain tropes and images, ethical and political evaluations. Here as in some other cases, Holocaust discourse functions like an international prism that helps focus the local discourse about the *desaparecidos* in both its legal and its commemorative aspects.

Thus from the very beginning of the official documentation of the dirty war waged by the military junta on its own population, the memory of the Holocaust has played an important role in the Argentinean discourse. The title of the first official collection of testimony, published in 1984 by CONADEP, the Argentine National Commission on the Disappeared, was *Nunca más* (*Never Again*), an explicit and emphatic reference to Holocaust discourse. The bombing of the Israeli embassy in Buenos Aires in 1992 and the impact in the following year of Steven Spielberg's film *Schindler's List* in Argentina represent other instances in which Holocaust memory made its mark on the internal Argentinean debate. And it is no coincidence that the scholarly memory debate emergent since the mid-1990s has drawn time and again on scholars of the Holocaust and has taken many of its cues from the international debate about Holocaust representations and commemoration.

What I mean by productive inscription of Holocaust discourse then is simply this: as in South Africa or again differently in Australia, the politics of Holocaust commemoration (what to remember, how to remember, when to remember), so prominent in the global media and in the countries of the northern transatlantic since the 1980s, has functioned like a motor energizing the discourses of memory elsewhere. There is reason to wonder whether without the prominence of Holocaust memory since the 1980s, most of the memory discourses the world over would be what they are today.[4]

Distinctions of course need to be made, but maybe we should hesitate before we lament the relativization of the Holocaust when it attaches itself like a floating signifier to historically very different situations. We should also be aware that references to the Holocaust may function as memory screens in radically opposing ways, either enabling a strong memory discourse and bringing a traumatic past to light or blocking any such public reckoning by insisting on the absolute incommensurability of the Holocaust with any other historical case. It is the uniqueness argument itself that may function in a politically relativizing way—relativizing, that is, atrocities committed in the present, post-Holocaust world (Bosnia, Rwanda, East Timor).

While much of the struggle for public memory in Argentina now transpires in the courts and focuses on reclaiming the identities of children born in captivity or kidnapped from their murdered parents, the emergent national debate about monuments, museums, and memorial sites is fast becoming the terrain on which Argentina grapples with its past and attempts to construct what Jan Assmann would call cultural memory.[5] Legal and cultural dimensions of this struggle thus reinforce and need each other. That is why the debate about a memory park within striking distance of the infamous ESMA, the Mechanical School of the Navy and a major torture chamber during the dirty war, can be indissolubly tied to claims articulated against members of the military in the courts and in the public sphere. Indeed, there was a debate about ESMA itself: whether to erase the building entirely, a proposal by President Menem that triggered massive public protest, or to transform it into a museum of the terror, which naturally met with strong opposition by the military. In the meantime, the Parque de la Memoria gains its symbolic weight in the context of ongoing legal struggles and the attempt to articulate a national memory of state terror. At the same time, its design itself speaks powerfully to the issue of the simultaneously global and local horizon of contemporary memory culture.

IV

As an observer from a distance and a non–Latin Americanist, I am not in a position to analyze the local controversy and public debate about the redesign of the *costanera norte*, the north shore and the university environs where the park is to be built, in all its historical and political depth.[6] But a few things must be said. The very project of the park itself has now become a bone of contention, not just, as to be expected, between the military and the regime's victims and their families, but among the opponents of that regime themselves who worry that the park may become just another figure for forgetting. Thus some oppose the park project because they wanted to transform the ESMA itself into a museum of the terror, a proposal whose time may come several decades from now at the earliest. Not surprisingly, the idea was stillborn. Others think that the park is too close to the ESMA and will therefore be shunned by those most directly affected by the terror. Yet others argue that projects such as the park or a museum would take away from the active political struggle still being waged by the Mothers and Grandmothers of the Plaza de Mayo. And then there are those for whom even a memory park is too much memory of the dictatorship. Clearly, this debate goes to the heart of Argentina's inescapable need to deal publicly with the legacies of state terrorism during the military dictatorship, a need that is exacerbated by the current financial and political crisis of the country. As such the debate about the memory park has become part of a complex local history of cover-up and amnesty, public protest and continuing legal struggle, and the nature of the park and what is to be commemorated in it has itself become a bone of contention.

At stake, as always in such cases, is the power of a commemorative site to keep the story alive as opposed to entombing it in the realm of the unspoken, of a past that is made to disappear yet once again.

Of course, many have written eloquently about the fraught question of how to represent historical trauma, how to find persuasive means of public remembrance, and how to construct monuments that evade the fate of imminent invisibility. How can such a monument be made to function as part of a network of urban relations, rather than standing disconnected from city life and ultimately referring only to itself? None of the various answers such as countermonuments, transitory monuments, or disappearing monuments can fully satisfy. Ultimately, the memory park project may not satisfy either, but the design for the "Monumento a las víctimas del terrorismo de Estado," a project of Baudizzone, Lestard, Varas Studio and the associated architects Claudio Ferrari and Daniel Becker, does raise a new dimension of commemorating national trauma in global context. Their design model, which won first prize in a competition of 1998, strikes me as one of the more interesting and potentially satisfactory solutions to this difficult problem.[7]

Many of the most compelling projects to nurture and to secure public memory involve interventions in urban space. This is only natural, because cities remain the main battleground on which societies articulate their sense of time past and time present. Once embodied in memorial sites as active parts within an urban fabric, remembrance of traumatic events seems less susceptible to the vagaries of memory. Memory thus has a chance to inscribe itself into history, to be codified into national consciousness. Cities, after all, are palimpsests of history, incarnations of time in stone, sites of memory extending both in time and space. The creation of an urban memorial site to a national trauma such as the Parque de la Memoria is a *lieu de mémoire* in a sense different from that advanced by Pierre Nora: it is a residue and reminder of a shameful and violent national past, more in the spirit of Derek Walcott, who wrote in his Caribbean epic *Omeros*: "the weight of cities that I found so hard to bear; in them was the terror of Time."[8] By resisting the desire to forget, the memorial as a site of

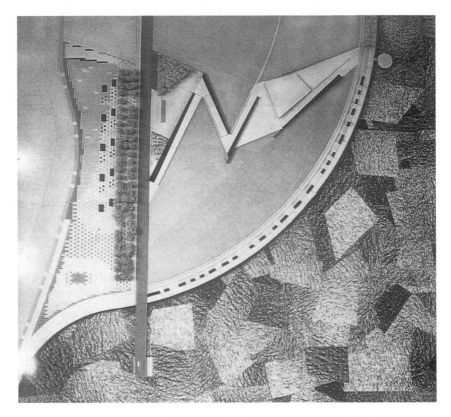

FIGURE 6.1 Monument to the Victims of the State Terror. Model. Courtesy Baudizzone, Lestard, Varas Studio, Buenos Aires.

intervention in the present may become an agent of political identity today. For memory is always of the present even though its ostensible content is of the past. Still one might ask: how can there be a memory consensus about a national trauma that pitted the majority of a society against a relatively small minority drawn from all ethnic and social backgrounds, that divided the national body into perpetrators and victims, beneficiaries and bystanders? The task just seems too daunting.

There are several closely connected reasons why the park's design is so persuasive and moving. The reasons are topographic, political, and aesthetic, and they do have a global dimension.

As already indicated, the park is located in the immediate neighborhood of the ESMA, which served as a central torture chamber of the military dictatorship, and it faces the river that carries such symbolic and historical significance for the citizens of Buenos Aires. The traditional meaning of the La Plata as a source of life is now overlaid by the fact that the river became the grave for hundreds of *desaparecidos*—its earthy brown, opaque waters a symbol of the unretrievability of drugged and tortured bodies, dumped from airplanes and swept out to the sea. Separated from the coastal road and from a set of university buildings by the straight line of a tree-lined pathway of slabs of colored concrete, the monument cuts deep into the elevated grassy surface of the park that faces the river in the half round. It is like a wound or a scar that runs the full diameter of the half circle in zigzag formation from the straight line of one walkway toward another paved path that frames the whole length of the park at the shore. Visitors will enter the monument underground from the city side of the wall, and move through the zigzag structure until the site releases them toward the river and the shoreline walkway. The open view toward the river is a key element in the design, which is classically modernist in its geometric configuration and felicitously minimalist in its lack of ornamentation and monumental ambition. It is thoroughly imbued with an aesthetic sensibility but never approaches the risk of aestheticizing traumatic memory. In its stylized simplicity of design it offers a place of reflection to its visitors—reflection on the relationship between river and city, history and politics.

What I have described as a wound cut into the earth is framed along its zigzag trajectory by four noncontinuous walls that will carry the names of the disappeared. The walls made of Patagonian porphyry are located each on only one side of the sloping walkway, thus creating perspective and guiding the gaze down the ramp rather than forcing the visitor to read turning back and forth from one side to the other. The highest elevation of the artificial elevation is six meters, and the lateral walls go down from four to one meters in height. There will be thirty thousand name plaques, and they will be sequenced alphabetically and by year. Many name plaques will remain empty, nameless, thus commemorating the violent voiding of identity that was the torturers' explicit goal and that always preceded disappearance. No doubt, more names will have to be added in years to come as the documentation of the state terror expands.

These walls with their inscribed names will document the extent of

FIGURE 6.2 Monument to the Victims of the State Terror. Model. Courtesy
Baudizzone, Lestard, Varas Studio, Buenos Aires.

state terror and provide a site for mourning, both personal and familial as
well as social and national. Naming names is an age-old and venerable
strategy of memorialization, but the naming in this monument is not of
the traditional heroic and martyrological kind. We are not remembering
heroes of war or martyrs for the fatherland. We are remembering students
and workers, women and men, ordinary people who had a social vision at
odds with that of the ruling elites, the church, and the military, a vision
shared by many young people across the globe at that time, but that led to
imprisonment, torture, rape, and death only in a few countries of the
world. Thus the memory park in Buenos Aires is more than a national

monument. It is also part of the global legacy of 1968, together with the mass shooting of students in Mexico City and the Soviet invasion of Czechoslovakia, perhaps its darkest and most tragic part.

V

This broader dimension of the memory of the terror is persuasively captured in the global resonances of the memorial's architecture and design. Sure, there is no explicit reference to the 1960s, nor is there any direct reference to the Holocaust. The memory park rather opens up to that global horizon by drawing on two contemporary icons of memory culture. For it cannot be a coincidence that it combines design elements of what to many people are two of the most successful memorial sites of recent decades: the Jewish Museum built in Berlin by Daniel Libeskind and the Vietnam Veterans Memorial (V.V.M.) designed by Maya Lin in Washington. Again, the point here is not to equate the terror of the Argentinean state with the Holocaust or with the American war in Vietnam, historical events that are widely different and occupy different spaces in history.[9] Rather, the powerful resonances open up a horizon that permits us to read the Argentinean case in the larger context of a now international culture of memory and its translation into building, memorial sites, and monuments.

Thus several features of the Libeskind museum and of the Lin memorial are creatively appropriated and transformed in the Varas monument. I emphasize the word *creative*, for it is not imitation that is at issue, but rather a new form of mimicry that acknowledges how local cultural discourses, be they political or aesthetic, are increasingly inflected by global conditions and practices. This was already true for the 1960s vision of a more equal and more just world beyond Cold War ideology, which took a heavy toll in the countries of the southern cone. And it is true again today in an age in which globalization produces new forms of locality that still have to find a vision of another future than that offered by neoliberalism, market ideology, and media triumphalism. Memory of past hopes, after all, remains part of any imagination of another future.

But let me get back to the monument's design and its resonances. To begin with, Libeskind called his Berlin building "between the lines."

The zigzag structure of the Jewish Museum is traversed by one straight line that gives architectural shape to the voids traversing the

FIGURE 6.3 The Berlin Museum with the Jewish Museum. Ground plan.
Courtesy Büro Daniel Libeskind.

museal space. The building asks to be read "between the lines." Architecture becomes script. Analogously, but quite differently, the Varas monument traverses a space between two lines, the straight line of the pedestrian
pathway separating the monument and the park from the city and the
round line that forms the other walkway along the shore. The monument
can then also be read between two lines, on one side of which you have the
city and on the other the river. Memory of the *desaparecidos* intervenes in

FIGURE 6.4 Maya Lin, Vietnam Veterans Memorial, Washington. Courtesy Architecture Slide Library, Columbia University.

between: between Buenos Aires and the La Plata river, but the space between the lines, the memory space, will always be fragile and depend on interpretation. It is a space for reading—reading the names on the walls and reading the past. Only when the visitor approaches the river will legibility end while the sense of disappearance takes over.

There are no architectural voids in the Varas design as there are in the Libeskind building. The voids or absences are in the life of the city and in the flow of the river, and they are marked on those name plaques that still remain empty. The zigzag structure itself, of course, evokes tortured discontinuity. Its discontinuous walls within, so different from the continuous mark of Maya Lin's angled walls, suggest fragmentation. And given that the monument is cut into the earth rather than rising above it as a building, it yields the additional emphatic sense of a wound to the earth or a scar to the body of the nation, much more so than the V.V.M. There is another resonance: both the Libeskind building and the Varas monument are to be entered from below—descent into the underworld, the world of specters, of painful memories that need to be preserved to secure the continuity and fu-

FIGURE 6.5   The Jewish Museum (1999). Courtesy Büro Daniel Libeskind.

ture of social life. The loss suffered can never be remedied, the wound will not heal, but the monument provides the space for the kind of reflection necessary to go on living and to feed the democratic public spirit.

The resonances with the V.V.M. are equally powerful. Both memorials are below surface level, though the Maya Lin structure in its simpler open-angled topography does not quite suggest the violations of a wound. More important, both sites feature walls with inscribed names that allow for personal and national mourning. In both, visitors are to walk along the trajectory of the walls that becomes a space for contemplation, perhaps prayer. It remains to be seen whether the monument in Buenos Aires will give rise to the same kind of moving popular dedication as the V.V.M.— with family members depositing flowers, pictures, letters, and candles near the names of those who lost their lives in an ultimately futile Cold War enterprise gone awry, a war that ended at about the same time that the Argentinean military began its murderous campaign of national purification and political cleansing.

Finally, another parallel links the Parque de la Memoria to the Jewish Museum in Berlin and the memorial in Washington. All three projects went through excruciatingly conflictive debates and drawn-out public controversy at the planning stage. In Washington such debate led to a hideous addition to Lin's minimalist and powerfully affective work, a blunt, figurative sculpture placed on a pedestal at the entrance to the V.V.M. that obviously satisfies the more traditional expectation of a *war* memorial. In Berlin it is too early to tell how, concretely, the Jewish Museum will function in the future, and the controversy over how to fill its exhibition halls is still in full swing. Only time will tell how the Monumento a las Victimas del Terrorismo de Estado will be accepted and used by the public. Although I don't quite share James Young's hyperbolic argument that the main benefit of any monument or memorial project may be the public debate it unleashes, I agree that such public debate is an essential component of success for any memorial project to take hold in the public sphere and to become part of a social and political imaginary. But the innumerable monuments in nineteenth-century style that litter the boulevards and public spaces of the city of Buenos Aires as of most European cities remind us, as the Austrian novelist Robert Musil once said, that nothing may be as invisible as a monument. What Musil had in mind, though, was figurative sculpture on a pedestal. That older practice, however, has been replaced by the preferred construction of memory sites in the expanded field that combine sculpture, landscaping, architecture, and design and their incorporation into an urban fabric. Aesthetic appeal, formal construction, and persuasive execution remain the sine qua non for a memory site to maintain a visible presence in the urban public sphere. To me, the Varas project fulfills those criteria. But it will be up to the Argentinean public to embrace it and to make it fulfill its ultimate purpose.

Doris Salcedo's Memory Sculpture:
Unland: The Orphan's Tunic

> A strange lostness was
> palpably present, almost
> you would
> have lived.
>
> —Paul Celan

In recent years, there's been the surprising emergence in post-minimalist art of what I would tentatively call memory sculpture: a kind of sculpture that is not centered on spatial configuration alone, but that powerfully inscribes a dimension of localizable, even corporeal memory into the work. This is an artistic practice that remains clearly distinct from the monument or the memorial. Its place is in the museum or the gallery rather than in public space. Its addressee is the individual beholder rather than the nation or the community. In its handling of materials and concepts, it relates to a specific tradition of installation art, and in its emphatic reliance on an experiential dimension it is much less confined by generic conventions than either the monument or the memorial would be. Monuments articulate official memory, and their fate inevitably is to be toppled or to become invisible. Lived memory, on the other hand, is always located in individual bodies, their experience and their pain, even when it involves collective, political, or generational memory. Anticipating Freud, Nietzsche acknowledged that simple fact when he said: "Only that which does not cease to hurt remains in memory." Sculpture expanded toward installation and incorporating memory traces relies on the traditions of the sculpted human body. In the works in question, however, the human body is never forgotten, though it is just as absent and elusive as it would be in any memory of the past.

Sculptures by artists such as Miroslav Balka from Poland, Ilja Kabakow from Russia, Rachel Whiteread from England, Vivan Sundaram from India, or Doris Salcedo from Colombia thus perform a kind of memory work that activates body, space, and temporality, matter and imagination, presence and absence in a complex relationship with their beholder. Their sheer presence counteracts our culture's triumphalism about media images and electronic immaterialization in virtual space, and they speak compellingly to the concerns with memory and absence that have emerged as dominant in the past decade or two. In these works, the material object is never just installation or sculpture in the traditional sense, but it is worked in such a way that it articulates memory as a displacing of past into present, offering a trace of a past that can be experienced and read by the viewer. It thus opens up an extended time-space challenging the viewer to move beyond the material presence of the sculpture in the museum and to enter into dialogue with the temporal and historical dimension implicit in the work. At the same time, these sculptures do not fall for the delusion of authenticity or pure presence. In the use of (often old or discarded) materials and their arrangement, they display an awareness that all memory is recollection, re-presentation. As opposed to much avant-garde artistic practice in this century then, this kind of work is not energized by the notion of forgetting. Its temporal sensibility is decidedly post-avant-garde. It fears not only the erasure of a specific (personal or political) past that may, of course, vary from artist to artist; it rather works against the erasure of pastness itself, which, in its projects, remains indissolubly linked to the materiality of things and bodies in time and space. I would like to suggest that the various forms of temporal and spatial displacements in the sculptures of artists such as Salcedo, Sundaram, Balka, and Whiteread mark a specific place in the broader culture of the 1990s, a culture that it would be frivolous and meaningless to call post-postmodern, but that is nevertheless significantly different from the postmodernism of the 1970s and 1980s. This is not to say that such memory sculptures are somehow "expressive" of some unified, totalizing *Zeitgeist*; despite a shared postminimalist language, these works are too different in terms of the politics, histories, and locales that gave rise to them. It is to suggest, however, that they are part of a larger problematic,

FIGURE 7.1 Doris Salcedo, *Unland: The Orphan's Tunic* (1997). Courtesy: Doris Salcedo.

which is the restructuring of the sense of space and time in our age of mass media, cyberspace, and globalization. Respecting the specificity of each individual artist's work, this essay focuses only on one outstanding example of what I call memory sculpture, a work by Doris Salcedo.

The work is one of three in a series of sculptures entitled *Unland* (1997), and first exhibited far from their place of origin, in the New Museum in New York City in 1998. If the land is the site of life and culture, of community and nation, then "unland" would be its radical negation. As a poetic neologism it implicitly retracts the promises contained in its linguistic kin "utopia," the no-place of an imagined alternative future. Thus far from embodying the imagination of another and better world, unland is the obverse of utopia, a land where even "normal" life with all its contradictions, pains and promises, happiness and miseries has become unlivable. As an artist working in a country that is being torn apart by a self-perpetuating cycle of violence and lawlessness, Salcedo leaves no doubt as to the identity of this unland that serves as her melancholy inspiration. It is her homeland, Colombia.

If such a reading of the work's title suggests an explicit and straight-forward political art practice, nothing could be further from the truth. Salcedo's sculpture captures the viewer's imagination in its unexpected, haunting visual and material presence in a way that does not easily relate to its mysterious title and subtitle, *Unland: The Orphan's Tunic*. The haunting effect is not there at first sight as the viewer approaches what from a distance looks like a simple, unremarkable table with some uneven surfaces. It comes belatedly, *nachträglich*, as Freud would say. It deepens as the viewer engages with the work. The muted but expressive power of this sculpture grows slowly; it depends on duration, on sustained contemplation, on visual, linguistic, and political associations woven together into a dense texture of understanding. And it raises the question of sculpture as material object in novel ways that sidestep the much debated issues of abstraction vs. figuration, objecthood vs. theatricalization, plastic action, or installation.

If classical sculpture captures the salient moment or crystallizes an idea or ideal form from the flow of time, then Salcedo's memory sculpture unlocks itself only within the flow of time because temporality itself is inscribed into the work. It dramatizes its materials, yet holds on to an emphatic notion of work, object, sculpture rather than dissolving work into performance. It embodies an expanded temporality, and as object it performs the process of memory. *The Orphan's Tunic* is objet trouvé, kitchen table, used and abused, material residue and witness. The object that appears simple and unassuming at first sight begins to come alive upon closer inspection. Its complexity has as much to do with what is there before the spectator's eyes as with what is absent. That which is *heimlich* and familiar, the everyday piece of furniture, becomes *unheimlich*, uncanny, but the homely is both preserved and denied in the *unheimlich*, just as land is in the Celan-inspired title of Unland. For one realizes that what looked like one table with different level surfaces is actually made up of two tables of different length, width, and height, violently jammed into each other, the smaller, somewhat wider and higher table shining in a whitish, luminous gray, the longer table dark brown with blackened marks of heavy use.

Both tables are mutilated. Where they clash and are mounted into each other, the inner two sets of legs are broken off.

As the spectator's gaze scans the surface, the whitish shine reveals itself to be a silk covering, the tunic, very thin natural silk that covers the surface and runs down the side boards and covers the two remaining legs.

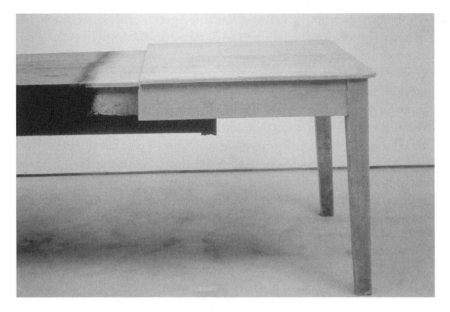

FIGURE 7.2 Doris Salcedo, *Unland: The Orphan's Tunic* (detail 1).
Courtesy Doris Salcedo.

The silk is so thin that the eye is drawn to the cracks visible underneath, gaps between the five wooden boards that make up the table's rather rough surface, and other smaller cracks and gouges attributable to the table's former use. The silk frays over the gap between the middle boards, suggesting perhaps that the table is still expanding, and it folds into some of the smaller cracks as if it were growing into them, attaching itself like a protective skin to the unevenness of the wood. Examining the surface of this table is like looking at the palm of a hand with its lines, folds, and wrinkles. The effect is closeness, intimacy, and at the same time a sense of fragility and vulnerability that contrasts with the sturdiness of the wooden table. Suddenly the table appears to be no more than a trace, a mute trace. But a trace that has now been so heavily worked over by the artist that it has acquired a powerful language. It speaks a language that is aesthetically complex without being aestheticizing, and subtly political without resorting to a direct message.

Salcedo's work on the homeliness of the kitchen table that has become the uncanny is not tied to individual psychology, nor are we merely dealing with a negative aesthetic in an Adornean or avant-gardist sense of distortion or defamiliarization. At stake is rather the conscious artistic translation of a national pathology of violence into a sculpture that articulates pain and defiance by bearing witness. The work is not simply there as object *in* the present, even though it is very much *of* the present. It leads the viewer back to some other time and space that is absent, yet subtly inscribed into the work: Celan's "strange lostness" that is "palpably present." Doris Salcedo's art is the art of the witness, the artist as secondary witness to be precise, the witness to lives and life stories of people forever scarred by the experience of violence that keeps destroying family, community, nation, and ultimately the human spirit itself.

For some years now, Salcedo has traveled the land, searching out and listening to the stories of people who have witnessed and survived gratu-

FIGURE 7.3 Doris Salcedo, *Unland: The Orphan's Tunic* (detail 2).
Courtesy Doris Salcedo.

itous violence directly, who have lost parents and siblings, spouses, friends, and neighbors to guerrillas, drug gangs, and military death squads. In the case of *The Orphan's Tunic*, as Salcedo tells it, it was the story of a girl from an orphanage, a six-year-old, who had witnessed the killing of her mother. Ever since that traumatic experience, she had been wearing the same dress day after day, a dress her mother had made for her shortly before being killed: the dress as a marker of memory and sign of trauma. The story forces us to take *The Orphan's Tunic* literally as index of a death, a life, a trauma, something that did happen in the real world. At the same time, *dress* is translated into *tunic* and becomes a metaphor for a child's loss and pain—a permanent marker of identity.

This metaphoric dimension is then put through another loop that adds to its texture. The choice of the word *tunic*, by way of an implicit *Eng-führung*, points to another Celan poem, a poem from *Lichtzwang*, a poem without title, orphaned, as it were.

> Night rode him, he had come to his senses,
>
> the orphan's tunic was his flag,
>
> no more going astray,
> it rode him straight—
>
> It is, it is as though oranges hung in the privet,
> as though the so-ridden had nothing on
> but his
> first
> birth-marked, se-
> cret-speckled
> skin.

The poem, fraying into Salcedo's work by way of the sculpture's sub-title, provides the linkage between tunic and skin, or between dress and body, a linkage that proves to be central for the aesthetic and material trans-position of event, idea, and concept into the finished work. Documentary investigation, poetry, and materials blend into the sculpture, which lives off its temporal dimension as much as it relies on its spatial presence.

This double temporal and spatial effect is heightened when, looking even closer, one notices the thousands of minuscule holes, many of them $1/4$ to $1/8$ inch apart, with human hair threaded through them, going down into the wood, resurfacing, and going in again. If the silk is marked from

FIGURE 7.4 Doris Salcedo, *Unland: The Orphan's Tunic* (detail 3).
Courtesy Doris Salcedo.

below by the unevenness and natural splits in the wood surface, it is marked
from above by hundreds of hairs that look like small pencil marks but actually hold the silk tunic close to the table. Now it is like looking at the
back of a hand and noticing the short, fine hair growing out of the skin.

If the tunic is like a skin—the "first/birth-marked, se-/cret-speckled
/skin"—then the table gains a metaphoric presence as body, not now of an
individual orphan but of an orphaned community deprived of a normal
life. Exhibited as memory sculpture far from its homeland in an international art world, this work appears itself orphaned and homeless in the
spaces it now occupies.

How are we to understand this combination of human hair and
wood? Both are material residues from formerly living organisms, now arrested in their growth. Clearly, the work plays on the contrast: the hair as
fragile, thin, and vulnerable, with reminiscences of the famous piles of hair
that we know from Holocaust photography, hair thus suggesting not life
but death. The wood of the table, on the other hand, is a solid, sturdy
guarantor of stability. But just as the hair has been cut, the tables have

been mutilated. Not the least of the various mutilations are the thousands of holes drilled through the surface with a $1/64$ drill bit before the hair could be stitched through. The very idea of the painstaking labor involved gives one pause. What an utterly absurd activity, stitching hair, and lots of it, through a wooden surface. But is it only absurd? Or is it perhaps also an act of mending? If the table stands for community, family, life in its temporal extension, then the stitching of hair, the inorganic trace of a human body, of the victim of violence, through the table's surface is like the threading of pain and its memories through the surface of history.

But perhaps the most stunning part of the sculpture is the thick band of hair that looks as if woven across the table just at the threshold between the silk tunic and the bare surface of the brown table. Here the tunic appears stitched down and held down by the hair, secured in place—hair, skin, texture, body, all come densely together in this part of the sculpture. It is close to where the two tables are jammed into each other, close to where the four middle legs have been broken off, the threshold that makes the table structure look vulnerable. Here it might cave in if pressure were applied from above. And precisely this tenuous threshold seems fortified by the band of hair, densely woven from one side of the table across to the other side and down on the side. It marks the end of the tunic on one side, the end of the barren brown surface on the other; it becomes thick texture. Hair appears here as providing strength, while the table seems vulnerable: an imaginative reversal of the basic nature of the materials. However absurd this project of stitching hair through wood is, it also has an air of defiance: it defies the implacability of the wood, but it also defies the absurdity and gratuitousness of violence in Colombia.

Like all of Salcedo's work, *The Orphan's Tunic* is about memory at the edge of an abyss. It is about memory in the literal sense, both the content of specific memories of violent acts and memory as process and as structure as the work enters into dialogue with the viewer. And it is about memory in a spatial sense, approximating it, never quite getting to it, compelling the viewer to innervate something that remains elusive, absent—the violent death of the mother that left the child orphaned, the orphan present only in that residual tunic, which now seems more like a shroud covering part of the table. Forever absent are the communal or family events that took place around this table, the chairs, the people, the food and drink served here. If the people, especially the indigenous people, belong to the land, as Salcedo has suggested in one of her rare interviews, then *Unland* marks the absence of the people from the communal site. But it is a forced absence achieved through death and displacement.

If *Unland: The Orphan's Tunic* is adequately seen as a memory sculpture, inevitably the question will arise: what of hope, what of redemption? And what kind of a politics of memory, if any, does Salcedo's artistic practice imply? Clearly, the work defies a politics of redemption, and it suggests defiance in an even broader sense: defiance first of any direct representation of a self-perpetuating violence it would be too legitimizing to call political; defiance also of an increasingly spectacularized culture of memory and its obsession with public sites of commemoration, monuments, and memorials. Salcedo knows how public monuments and memorials are bound to serve as ciphers of forgetting through aestheticization or direct political comment. Her work does not trust mechanisms of public memory, while at the same time it desperately desires to nurture such memory. This is the minimal hope the work does suggest. Sculptural form, rather than monument or memorial, the work addresses the individual spectator, inscribes its complex message, and leaves the spectator moved by the memory of a powerful image. But the reality of *la violencia*, we know, continues unabated. There is no end in sight for the cycle of violence that feeds on itself in Colombia, like Chronos devouring his own children in Greek myth.

Finally, there is Salcedo's defiance—or should one say overcoming—of the always present danger of aestheticization, due primarily to her use of simple, everyday objects and materials. And yet, even if our gaze is not arrested in aesthetic pleasure, *Unland: The Orphan's Tunic* haunts us in its compelling beauty. As in other successful artistic work articulating historical trauma in unique media and materials, Salcedo's sculpture moves the spectator to the edge of an abyss only thinly veiled by the beauty of the piece itself. The veil, however, is indispensable for us to come face to face with the trauma and to become witnesses of a history we must not ignore.

Memory sculptures such as the ones by Doris Salcedo are currently being produced in many different places in the world—in India and South Africa, in the countries of the former Soviet bloc and in Latin America. The works may be influenced and coded to varying degrees by the Western art system, which is itself becoming global, but the inscribed traditions and memories will be invariably local and space-bound, challenging the beholder to engage with them. The demise of the Euro-American model privileging the latest avant-garde actually facilitates a hybrid merging of different times and different spaces in artistic practices and their reception. The geographic and temporal splintering of contemporary art will of course generate problems of legibility when such works are then exhibited in other places that have other histories. But then art has always interacted beneficially with ways of reading, commentary, and interpretation that could become generative of the spectator's dialogue with the work. Reading in a globalizing culture requires new skills and new knowledge, and works such as Salcedo's foster a dialogue beyond the frontiers of "Western" art.

But apart from the invariably specific histories, localities, and corporeal memories that the works ask the beholder to trace, as a medium by itself memory sculpture asserts the need for a slowdown, and it demands recognition of the basic matter of everyday life. As sculpture it insists on the insuperable materiality of the world, of objects as well as of bodies. Its inscriptions of time and displacements of space need to be read patiently. They are usually not to be found on the surface, in the way of documentary or politically explicit art. This complicates reception. The viewer may have to rely as much on association, analogy, innervation of the work as on explanations that may or may not be offered with captions, catalogues, and reviews. Primarily, of course, the artists will want to get to the imagination of the viewer through the language of their materials, the suggestiveness of markings, the uses of space and configuration. If the work is successful in engaging the attentiveness of the beholder, if it suggests meaning yet refuses easy consumption, if it yields pleasure in its aesthetic configuration without denying cognitive gain, then it does its job. It works against the structures of forgetfulness in our contemporary world, whether such forgetfulness is enforced by a military state and its system of "disappearing" people (Salcedo), triggered by the transformation of a formerly communist society in which public and private remembrance and forgetting are thrown into turmoil (Balka or Kabakow), or simply brought about by the planned obsolescence of objects (and people?) in the consumerism of our own Western societies. Such art also contests the draining of space and time in hyperspace. It nurtures the basic human need to live in extended structures of temporality and in recognizable space, however they may be organized. And it enriches the beholder by drawing us into its slow work on the indissoluble relationship among space, memory, and bodily experience. Luis Buñuel once said: "You have to begin to lose your memory, if only in bits and pieces, to realize that memory is what makes our lives." The art of Doris Salcedo and others working on memory and space in sculpture and installations helps us not to forget that and, perhaps, to look with fresh eyes at the way we ourselves negotiate space and memory in our own everyday lives.

Of Mice and Mimesis: Reading Spiegelman with Adorno

> I resist becoming the Elie
> Wiesel of the comic book.
>
> —Art Spiegelman

Since the 1980s, the question no longer is *whether* but rather *how* to represent the Holocaust in literature, film, and the visual arts. The earlier conviction about the essential unrepresentability of the Holocaust, typically grounded in Adorno's famous statement about the barbarism of poetry after Auschwitz and still powerful in some circles today, has lost much of its persuasiveness for later generations who know of the Holocaust only through representations to begin with: photos and films, documentaries, testimonies, historiography, and fiction. Given the flood of Holocaust representations in all manner of media today, it would be sheer voluntarism to stick with Adorno's aesthetic requirement of a ban on images that translates a theological concept into a very specific kind of modernist aesthetic. It seems much more promising to approach the issue of Holocaust representations through another concept that holds a key place in Adorno's thought, that of mimesis.

In his recently published book entitled *In the Shadow of Catastrophe: German Intellectuals between Apocalypse and Enlightenment,*[1] Anson Rabinbach has persuasively shown how Adorno's understanding of Nazi anti-Semitism is energized by his theory of mimesis.[2] More important, however, he has linked Adorno's discussion of the role of mimesis in anti-Semitism to Horkheimer and Adorno's historical and philosophical reflections on mimesis as part of the evolution of signifying systems, as they are elaborated in the first chapter of the *Dialectic of Enlightenment*.[3] Here Horkheimer and Adorno discuss mimesis in its true and repressed forms, its role in the process of civilization and its paradoxical relationship to the *Bilderverbot*, the prohibition of graven images.[4] At the same time, the concept of mimesis in Adorno (and I take it that Adorno rather than Horkheimer was the driving force in articulating this concept in the co-authored work) is not easily defined, as several recent studies have shown.[5] It actually functions more like a palimpsest in that it partakes in at least five different yet overlapping discursive registers in the text: first in relation to the critique of the commodity form, its powers of reification and deception, a thoroughly negative form of mimesis (*Mimesis ans Verhärtete*); second, in relation to the anthropological grounding of human nature that, as Adorno insists in *Minima Moralia*, is "indissolubly linked to imitation";[6] third, in a biological somatic sense geared toward survival as Adorno had encountered it in Roger Caillois's work, some of which he reviewed for the *Zeitschrift für Sozialforschung*;[7] fourth, in the sense of identification and projection indebted to Freud's *Totem and Taboo*; and last, in an aesthetic sense and with strong resonances of Benjamin's language theory, in relation to the role of word and image in the evolution of signifying systems. It is precisely this multivalence of mimesis, I would argue, that makes the concept productive for contemporary debates about memory, trauma, and representation in the public realm. Thus it is more than merely a paradox that mimesis serves Adorno to read Nazi anti-Semitism, whereas it serves me to understand the ethics and aesthetics of approaching Holocaust memory in our time.

In this essay, then, I will focus on one specific aspect of memory discourse, namely, the vexing issue of (in Timothy Garton Ash's succinct words) if, how, and when to represent historical trauma.[8] My example for the representation of historical trauma is the Holocaust, a topic on which, as already indicated, Adorno had provocative things to say, although he never said quite enough about it. But the issues raised in this essay pertain as much to other instances of historical trauma and their representation: whether we think of the *desaparecidos* in Argentina, Guatemala, or Chile, the stolen generation in Australia, or the post-apartheid debates in South Africa—in all these cases issues of how to document, how to represent, and how to view and listen to testimony about a traumatic past have powerfully emerged in the public domain.

I hope to show that a reading through mimesis of one specific Holocaust image-text may allow us to go beyond arguments focusing primarily on the rather confining issue of how to represent the Holocaust "properly" or how to avoid aestheticizing it. My argument will be based on the reading of a work that has shocked many precisely because it seems to violate the *Bilderverbot* in the most egregious ways, but that has also been celebrated, at least by some, as one of the most challenging in an ever-widening body of recent works concerned with the Holocaust and its remembrance. But more is at stake here than just the reading of one work through the conceptual screen of another. A discussion of Art Spiegelman's *Maus*[9] in terms of the mimetic dimension may get us beyond a certain kind of stalemate in debates about representations of the Holocaust, a stalemate that, ironically, rests on presuppositions that were first and powerfully articulated by Adorno himself in a different context and at a different time. Reading *Maus* through the conceptual screen of mimesis will permit us to read Adorno against one of the most lingering effects of his work on contemporary culture, the thesis about the culture industry and its irredeemable link with deception, manipulation, domination, and the destruction of subjectivity. While this kind of uncompromising critique of consumerist culture, linked as it is to a certain now historical type of modernist aesthetic practice, resonates strongly with a whole set of situationist and post-structuralist positions developed in France in the 1960s (Barthes, Debord, Baudrillard, Lyotard, Tel Quel), it has generally been on the wane in contemporary aesthetic practices. For obvious reasons, however, it has proven to have much staying power in one particular area: that of Holocaust representations, where Adorno's statements about poetry after Auschwitz (often misquoted, unanalyzed, and ripped out of their historical context)[10] have become a standard reference point and have fed into the recent revival of notions of an aesthetic sublime and its dogmatic antirepresentational stance.[11] But this is where the issue of public memory emerges. Politically, most everybody seems to agree, the genocide of the Jews is to be remembered (with allegedly salutary effects on present and future) by as large a public as possible, but mass cultural representations are not considered proper or correct. The paradigmatic case exemplifying this broad, though now perhaps fraying, consensus is the debate over Spielberg's *Schindler's List* and Lanzmann's *Shoah*. Spielberg's film, playing to mass audiences, fails to remember properly because it represents, thus fostering forgetting: Hollywood as fictional substitute for "real history." Lanzmann's refusal to represent, on the other hand, is said to embody memory in the proper way precisely because it avoids the delusions of a presence of that which is to be remembered. Lanzmann's film is praised as something like a heroic effort in the Kulturkampf against the memory industry, and its refusal to re-present, its adherence to *Bilderverbot*, becomes the ground for its authenticity.[12] Aesthetically speaking, these opposing validations of Spielberg vs. Lanzmann still rest on the unquestioned modernist dichotomy that pits Hollywood and mass culture against forms of high art.[13] Looking at Spiegelman's *Maus* through the various discursive screens of mimesis, I want to argue, may allow us to approach Holocaust memory and its representations today in a way that is different from this earlier dominant paradigm.

Maus undercuts this dichotomy in the first, rather obvious, sense that Spiegelman draws on the comic book as a mass cultural genre, but transforms it in a narrative saturated with modernist techniques of self-reflexivity, self-irony, ruptures in narrative time, and highly complex image sequencing and montaging. As a comic, *Maus* resonates less with Disney than with a whole tradition of popular animal fables from Aesop to La Fontaine and even Kafka. At the same time, it evolved from an American comic book countertradition born in the 1960s that includes works such as *Krazy Kat, Fritz the Cat,* and others. At the same time, *Maus* remains different from the older tradition of the enlightening animal fable. If the animal fable (George Orwell's novel *Animal Farm* is a twentieth-century example) had enlightenment as its purpose either through satire or moral instruction, *Maus* remains thoroughly ambiguous, if not opaque, as to the possible success of such enlightenment. Rather than providing us with an enlightened moral or with a happy reconciliation between high and low, human and animal, trauma and memory, the aesthetic and emotional effect of *Maus* remains jarring throughout. This jarring, irritating effect on the reader results from a variety of pictorial and verbal strategies that have their common vanishing point in mimesis, both in its insidious and in its salutary aspects that, as Adorno would have it, can never be entirely separated from each other.

Let me turn now to some of the dimensions of mimesis in this image-text. As is well known, *Maus* as narrative is based on interviews Art Spiegelman conducted with his father, Vladek, an Auschwitz survivor, in the 1970s. Spiegelman taped these interviews in Rego Park, Queens, in the house in which he grew up and during a summer vacation in the Catskills. The subject of these interviews is the story of Spiegelman's parents' life in Poland in the years 1933–44, but the telling of this traumatic past, as retold in the comic, is interrupted time and again by banal everyday events in the New York present. This crosscutting of past and present, by which the frame keeps intruding into the narrative, allows Spiegelman to have it both ways: for Vladek, it seems to establish a safe distance between the two temporal levels; actually the tale of his past is visually framed by Spiegelman as if it were a movie projected by Vladek himself. As Vladek begins to tell his story, pedaling on his exercycle, he says proudly: "People always told me I looked just like Rudolph Valentino" (I:13). Behind him in the frame is a large poster of Valentino's 1921 film *The Sheik* with the main actor as a mouse holding a swooning lady in his arms, and the whole exercycle mechanism looks remotely like a movie projector with the spinning wheel resembling a film reel and Vladek, as narrator, beginning to project his story. But simultaneously this crosscutting of past and present points in a variety of ways to how this past holds the present captive independently of whether this knotting of past into present is being talked about or repressed. Thus one page earlier, Art, who is sitting in the background and has just asked Vladek to tell him the story of his life in Poland before and during the war, is darkly framed within the frame by his father's arms and the exercycle's handlebars in the foreground. Vladek's arms, head, and shirt with rolled-up sleeves are all striped, and the Auschwitz number tattooed into his left arm hovers ominously just above Art's head in the frame (I:12). Both the narrator (Art Spiegelman) and the reader see Vladek's everyday behavior permeated by his past experiences of persecution during the Nazi period. And then this first narrative framing is itself split in two. In addition to the narrative frame the interviews provide, there is yet another level of narrative time that shows the author Art Spiegelman, or rather the *Kunstfigur* Artie, during his work on the book in the years 1978 to 1991, years during which Vladek Spiegelman died and the first part of *Maus* became a great success, all of which is in turn incorporated into the narrative of the second volume. But the complexity of the narration is not just an aesthetic device employed for its own sake. It rather results from the desire of the second generation to learn about their parents' past, of which they are always, willingly or not, already a part: it is a project of

mimetically approximating historical and personal trauma in which the
various temporal levels are knotted together in such a way that any talk
about a past that refuses to pass away or that should not be permitted to
pass, as discussed in the German *Historikerstreit* of the mid-1980s, seems
beside the point.[14] The survivors' son's life stands in a mimetic affinity to
his parents' trauma long before he ever embarks on his interviews with his
father.[15] Therefore this mimetic relationship cannot be thought of simply
as a rational and fully articulated working through.[16] There are dimensions
to mimesis that lie outside linguistic communication and that are locked
in silences, repressions, gestures, and habits—all produced by a past that
weighs all the more heavily as it is not (yet) articulated. Mimesis in its
physiological, somatic dimension is *Angleichung,* a becoming or making
similar, a movement toward, never a reaching of, a goal. It is not identity,
nor can it be reduced to compassion or empathy. It rather requires us to
think identity and nonidentity together as nonidentical similitude and in
unresolvable tension with each other.

Maus performs precisely such a mimetic approximation. Spiegelman's
initial impetus for conducting these interviews with his father came itself
out of a traumatic experience: the suicide of his mother, Anja, in 1968, an
event Spiegelman made into a four-page image text originally published in
1973 in an obscure underground comic under the title "Prisoner of the Hell
Planet." It is only in the latter half of the first part of *Maus* that Artie suddenly and unexpectedly comes across a copy of this earlier, now almost forgotten attempt to put part of his own life's story into the comics. *Maus* then
reproduces the "Prisoner of the Hell Planet" in toto (I:100–103). These four
pages, all framed in black like an obituary in German newspapers, intrude
violently into the mouse narrative, breaking the frame in three significant
ways. First, in this earlier work, the figures of Vladek and Artie mourning
the death of Anja are drawn as humans, a fact that goes surprisingly unre-
marked by the mice Artie and Vladek as they are looking at these pages in
the narrative of the later work. The identity of the nonidentical seems to be
taken for granted in this porousness between human and animal realm. Sec-
ondly, the comic "Prisoner of the Hell Planet" opens with a family photo
that shows ten-year-old Art in 1958 with his mother on summer vacation in
the Catskills.[17] It is the first of altogether three family photos montaged into
the comic, all of which function not to document but to stress the unassim-
ilability of traumatic memory.[18] Third, "Prisoner" articulates an extreme

moment of unadulterated despair that disrupts the "normal" frame of the interviewing process, the questioning and answering, bickering and fighting between father and son. These pages give testimony of the emotional break-down of both father and son at Anja's burial: in Art's case, it is overlaid by a kind of survivor guilt in the second degree, once removed from the original trauma of his parents. The memories of Auschwitz do not only claim Anja; they also envelop the son born years after the war. Thus Art draws himself throughout this episode in striped Auschwitz prisoner garb, which gives a surreal quality to these starkly executed, woodcut-like, grotesque images. In this moment of secondary Holocaust trauma Spiegelman performs a kind of spatial mimesis of death in the sense of Roger Caillois's work of the 1930s, which Adorno read and commented on critically in his correspondence with Benjamin.[19] Spiegelman performs a compulsive imaginary mimesis of Auschwitz as a space of imprisonment and murder, a mimesis, however, in which the victim, the mother, becomes a perpetrator while the real perpe-trators have vanished. Thus at the end of this raw and paralyzing passage, Art, incarcerated behind imaginary bars, reproaches his mother for having committed the perfect crime: "You put me here . . . shorted all my cir-cuits . . . cut my nerve endings . . . and crossed my wires! . . . / You MUR-DERED me, Mommy, and you left me here to take the rap!!!" (I:103). The drawings are expressionist, the text crude though in a certain sense "authen-tic," but it is easy to see that Spiegelman's comic would have turned into disaster had he chosen the image and language mode of "Prisoner" for the later work. It could only have turned into psycho-comikitsch. Spiegelman did need a different, more estranging mode of narrative and figurative rep-resentation to overcome the paralyzing effects of a mimesis of memory-terror. He needed a pictorial strategy that would maintain the tension be-tween the overwhelming reality of the remembered events and the tenuous, always elusive status of memory itself. But as an insert in *Maus*, these pages function as a reminder about the representational difficulties of telling a Holocaust or post-Holocaust story in the form of the comic. But they also powerfully support Spiegelman's strategy to use animal imagery in the later, longer work. The choice of medium, the animal comic, is thus self-consciously enacted and justified in the narrative itself. Drawing the story of his parents and the Holocaust as an animal comic is the Odyssean cunning that allows Spiegelman to escape from the terror of memory—even "post-memory" in Marianne Hirsch's sense—while mimetically reenacting it.

But the question lingers. What do we make of the linguistic and pictorial punning of Maus, Mauschwitz, and the Catskills in relation to mimesis? The decision to tell the story of Germans and Jews as a story of cats and mice as predators and prey should not be misread as a naturalization of history, as some have done. Spiegelman is not the Goldhagen of the comic book. After all, the comic does not pretend to be history. More serious might be another objection: Spiegelman's image strategies problematically reproduce the Nazi image of the Jew as vermin, as rodent, as mouse. But is it simply a mimicry of racist imagery? And even if mimicry, does mimicry of racism invariably imply its reproduction, or can such mimicry itself open up a gap, a difference that depends on who performs the miming and how? Mimesis, after all, is based on similitude as making similar (*Angleichung* in Adorno's terminology), the production of "the same but not quite," as Homi Bhabha describes it in another context.[20] And *Angleichung* implies difference. Thus Spiegelman himself draws the reader's attention to his conscious mimetic adoption of this imagery. The very top of *Maus* I's copyright page features a Hitler quote: "The Jews are undoubtedly a race, but they are not human." And *Maus* II, right after the copyright page, begins with a motto taken from a Pomeranian newspaper article from the mid-1930s:

Mickey Mouse is the most miserable ideal ever revealed. . . . Healthy emotions tell every independent young man and every honorable youth that the dirty and filth-covered vermin, the greatest bacteria carrier in the animal kingdom, cannot be the ideal type of animal. . . . Away with Jewish brutalization of the people! Down with Mickey Mouse! Wear the Swastika Cross!

Maus thus gives copyright where it is due: Adolf Hitler and the Nazis.

But that may still not be enough as an answer to the objection. More crucial is the way in which the mimesis of anti-Semitic imagery is handled. Here it would be enough to compare Spiegelman's work with the 1940 Nazi propaganda movie *The Eternal Jew*, which portrayed the Jewish world conspiracy as the invasive migration of plague-carrying swarms of rodents who destroy everything in their path. Such a comparison makes it clear how Spiegelman's mimetic adoption of Nazi imagery actually succeeds in reversing its implications while simultaneously keeping us aware of the humiliation and degradation of that imagery's original intention. Instead of the literal representation of destructive vermin, we see persecuted little animals drawn with a human body and wearing human clothes and with a highly abstracted, nonexpressive mouse physiognomy. "Maus" here means vulnerability, unalloyed suffering, victimization. As in the case of the "Prisoner of the Hell Planet," here, too, an earlier, much more naturalistic version of the mouse drawings shows how far Spiegelman has come in his attempt to transform the anti-Semitic stereotype for his purposes by eliminating any all-too-naturalistic elements from his drawings.

Defenders of *Maus* have often justified the use of animal imagery as a necessary distancing device, a kind of Brechtian estrangement effect. Spiegelman's own justification is more complex:

First of all, I've never been through anything like that—knock on whatever is around to knock on—and it would be a counterfeit to try to pretend that the drawings are representations of something that's actually happening. I don't know exactly what a German looked like who was in a specific small town doing a specific thing. My notions are born of a few scores of photographs and a couple of movies. I'm bound to do something inauthentic. Also, I'm afraid that if I did it with people, it would be very corny. It would come out as some kind of odd plea for sympathy or 'Remember the Six Million,' and that wasn't my point exactly, either. To use these ciphers, the cats and mice, is actually a way to allow you past the cipher at the people who are experiencing it. So it's really a much more direct way of dealing with the material.[21]

This is, in my terms, an estrangement effect in the service of mimetic approximation, and thus rather un-Brechtian, for at least in his theoretical reflections, Brecht would not allow for any mimetic impulse in reception. Spiegelman accepts that the past is visually not accessible through realistic representation: whatever strategy he might choose, it is bound to be "inauthentic." He also is aware of his generational positioning as someone who mainly knows of this past through media representations. Documentary *authenticity* of representation can therefore not be his goal, but *authentication* through the interviews with his father is. The use of mice and cats is thus not simply an avant-gardist distancing device in order to give the reader a fresh, critical, perhaps even "transgressive" view of the Holocaust intended to attack the various pieties and official memorializations that have covered it discursively. Of course, Spiegelman is very aware of the dangers of using Holocaust memory as a screen memory for various political purposes in the present. His narrative and pictorial strategy is precisely devised to avoid that danger. It is actually a strategy of another kind of mimetic approximation: getting past the cipher at the people and their experience. But before getting past the cipher, Spiegelman has to put himself into that very system of ciphering: as Artie in the comic, he himself becomes a mouse, imitates the physiognomic reduction of his parents by racist stereotype, the post-Auschwitz Jew still as mouse, even though living now in the country of the dogs (America) rather than that of the cats. Paradoxically, we have here a mimetic approximation of the past that respects the *Bilderverbot* not despite, but rather because of its use of animal imagery, which tellingly avoids the representation of the human face. *Bilderverbot* and mimesis are no longer irreconcilable opposites but enter into a complex relationship in which the image is precisely not mere mirroring, ideological duplication, or partisan reproduction, but where it approaches writing.[22] This Adornean notion of image becoming script was first elaborated by Miriam Hansen and Gertrud Koch in their attempts to make Adorno pertinent to film theory.[23] But it works for Spiegelman's *Maus* as well. As its image track becomes script, *Maus* acknowledges the inescapable inauthenticity of Holocaust representations in the "realistic" mode, but it achieves a new and unique form of authentication and effect on the reader precisely by way of its complex layering of historical facts, their oral retelling, and their transformation into image-text. Indeed, it is as animal comic that *Maus* (to quote a typically Adornean turn of phrase from the first chapter of *Dialectic of Enlightenment*) "preserves the legitimacy of the image . . . in the faithful pursuit of its prohibition."[24]

If this seems too strong a claim, consider the notion of image becoming script in *Maus* from another angle. Again, Spiegelman himself is a good witness for what is at stake:

I didn't want people to get too interested in the drawings. I wanted them to be there, but the story operates somewhere else. It operates somewhere between the words and the idea that's in the pictures and in the movement between the pictures, which is the essence of what happens in a comic. So by not focusing you too hard on these people you're forced back into your role as reader rather than looker.[25]

And in a radio interview of 1992, he put it even more succinctly by saying that *Maus* is "a comic book driven by the word."[26]

I cannot hope to give a full sense of how the linguistic dimension of *Maus* drives the image sequences. A few comments will have to suffice. Central here is the rendering of Vladek's language taken from the taped interviews. The estranging visualization of the animal comic is counterpointed by documentary accuracy in the use of Vladek's language. The gestus of Vladek's speech, not easily forgotten by any reader with an open ear, is shaped by cadences, syntax, and intonations of his Eastern European background. His English is suffused by the structures of Yiddish. Residues of a lost world are inscribed into the language of the survivor immigrant. It is this literally—rather than poetically or mystically—broken speech that carries the burden of authenticating that which is being remembered or narrated. On the other hand, Vladek himself is aware of the problematic nature of any Holocaust remembrance, even in language, when he says: "It's no more to speak" (II:113). Spiegelman's complex arrangement of temporal levels finds its parallel in an equally complex differentiation of linguistic registers. Thus the inside narration about the years in Poland as told by Vladek are rendered in fluent English. A natural language gestus is required here because at that time Vladek would have spoken his national language, Polish. It is thus logical that Vladek's broken speech appears only on the level of the frame story, the narrative time of the present. Past and present, clearly distinguished by the language track, are thus nevertheless suffused in the present itself in Vladek's broken English, which provides the linguistic marker of the insuperable distance that still separates Artie from Vladek's experiences and from his memories. Artie, after all, always speaks fluent English as his native language.

If Spiegelman's project is mimetic approximation not of the events themselves, but of the memories of his parents, and thus a construction of his own "postmemory" (Marianne Hirsch), then this mimesis must remain fractured, frustrated, inhibited, incomplete. The pain of past trauma is repeated through narration in the present and attaches itself to the listener, to Artie as listener inside the text as well as to the reader who approaches the contents of Vladek's autobiographic tale through its effects on Artie. Artie as a *Kunstfigur*—the same but not quite the same as the author Art Spiegelman—thus becomes the medium in the text through which we ourselves become witnesses of his father's autobiographic narration. While this narration, gently and sometimes not so gently extracted from the survivor, aims at a kind of working-through in language, it is a mimetic process that will never reach an end or come to completion, even if Vladek's tale catches up to the postwar period. And then there is always that other most painful obstacle to a full mimetic knowledge of the past. For the process of an *Angleichung ans Vergangene*, an assimilation to the past, is not only interrupted by the inevitable intrusion of everyday events during the time of the interviews; another even more significant gap opens up in the sense that only Vladek's memories are accessible to Artie. The memories of Artie's mother, whose suicide triggered Art Spiegelman's project in the first place, remain inaccessible not only because of her death, but because Vladek, in a fit of despair after her death, destroyed her diaries, in which she had laid down her own memories of the years in Poland and in Auschwitz. And just as Artie had accused his mother for murdering him, he now accuses his father for destroying the diaries: "God DAMN you! You . . . you murderer!" (I:159). Anja's silence thus is total. If it was Anja's suicide that generated Art Spiegelman's desire to gain self-understanding through mimetic approximation of his parents' story and of survivor guilt, then the discovery that the diaries have been burned points to the ultimate elusiveness of the whole enterprise. Artie's frustration about the destruction of the diaries only makes explicit that ultimate unbridgeable gap that exists between Artie's cognitive desires and the memories of his parents. Indeed it marks the limits of mimetic approximation, but it marks them in a pragmatic way and without resorting to sublime new definitions of the sublime as the unpresentable within representation.

All of Spiegelman's strategies of narration thus maintain the insuperable tension within mimetic approximation between closeness and distance, affinity and difference. *Angleichung* is precisely not identification or simple compassion. Listening to his father's story makes Artie understand how Vladek's whole habitus has been shaped by Auschwitz and the struggle for survival, while Vladek himself, caught in traumatic reenactments, may remain oblivious to that fact: rather than assuming continuity, Vladek's storytelling seems to assume a safe and neutralizing distance between the events of the past and his New York present. But his concrete behavior constantly proves the opposite. Artie, on the other hand, is always conscious of the fact that the borders between past and present are fluid, not only in his observation of his father, but in his self-observation as well. Mimetic approximation as a self-conscious project thus always couples closeness and distance, similitude and difference.

This dimension becomes most obvious in those passages in *Maus* II where Spiegelman draws himself drawing *Maus* (II:41ff.). The year is 1987; Vladek has been dead for five years; Art works on *Maus* II from the tapes that now have become archive; and *Maus* I has become a great commercial success. This chapter, entitled "Auschwitz (Time Flies)," demonstrates how beyond the multiply fractured layering of language and narrative time, the very pictoriality of the animal comic is significantly disrupted as well. We see Art in profile, sitting at his drawing table, but now drawn as a human figure wearing a mouse mask. It is as if the image track could no longer sustain itself, as if it had collapsed under its own weight. Artie's mimicry reveals itself to be a sham. The mask reveals the limits of his project. The ruse doesn't work any longer. The task of representing time in Auschwitz itself, just begun in the preceding chapter, has reached a crisis point. This crisis in the creative process is tellingly connected with the commercial success of *Maus* I: the Holocaust as part of the culture industry. Crisis of representation and crisis of success throw the author into a depressive melancholy state in which he resists the marketing of his work (translations, film version, TV) through a fit of total regression. He avoids the annoying questions of the media sharks (such as: What is the message of your book? Why should younger Germans today feel guilty? How would you draw the Israelis? II:42) by literally shrinking in his chair from frame to frame until we see a small child screaming: "I want . . . I want . . . my Mommy!" (II:42). The pressures of historical memory are only intensified by Holocaust marketing, to the point where the artist refuses any further communication. The culture industry's obsession with the Holocaust almost succeeds in shutting down Spiegelman's quest. The desire for a regression to childhood, as represented in this sequence, however, is not only an attempt to cope with the consequences of commercial success and to avoid the media. This moment of extreme crisis, as close as any in the work to traumatic silence and refusal to speak, also anticipates something of the very ending of *Maus* II.

On the very last page of *Maus* II, as Vladek's story has caught up with his postwar reunification with Anja, ironically described by Vladek in Hollywood terms as a happy ending and visually rendered as the irislike fade-out at the end of silent films, Artie is again put in the position of a child.[27] In a case of mistaken identity resulting from a merging of past and present in his father's mind, Vladek addresses Artie as Richieu, Artie's own older brother who did not survive the war, whose only remaining photo had always stared at him reproachfully during his childhood from the parents' bedroom wall, and to whom *Maus* II is dedicated. As Vladek asks Artie to turn off his tape recorder and turns over in his bed to go to sleep, he says to Artie: "I'm tired from talking, Richieu, and it's enough stories for now . . . " (II:136). This misrecognition of Artie as Richieu is highly ambiguous: it is as if the dead child had come alive again, but simultaneously the traumatic past proves its deadly grip over the present one last time. For these are the last words a dying Vladek addresses to Artie. This last frame of the comic is followed only by an image of a gravestone with Vladek's and Anja's names and dates inscribed and, at the very bottom of the page and below the gravestone, by the signature "art spiegelman 1978–1991," years that mark the long trajectory of Spiegelman's project of approaching an experience that ultimately remains beyond reach.

Much more could be said about Spiegelman's mimetic memory project, but I hope to have made the case that the Adornean category of mimesis can be made productive in a reading of Holocaust remembrance in such a way that the debate about the proper or correct Holocaust representation, while perhaps never irrelevant, can be bracketed and the criteria of judgment shifted. If mimetic approximation, drawing on a variety of knowledges (historical, autobiographic, testimonial, literary, museal), were to emerge as a key concern, then one could look at other Holocaust representations through this prism rather than trying to construct a Holocaust canon based on narrow aesthetic categories pitting the unrepresentable against aestheticization, or modernism against mass culture, memory against forgetting. This might open up a field of discussion more productive than the ritualistic incantations of Adorno regarding the culture industry or the barbarity of poetry after Auschwitz.

As a work by a member of the "second generation," *Maus* may mark a shift in the ways in which the Holocaust and its remembrance are now represented. It is part of a body of newer, "secondary" attempts to commemorate the Holocaust while simultaneously incorporating the critique of representation and staying clear of official Holocaust memory and its rituals. I have tried to show how Spiegelman confronts the inauthenticity of representation within a mass cultural genre while at the same time telling an autobiographic story and achieving a powerful effect of authentication. Like many other works of film, sculpture, monuments, literature, theater, even architecture, Spiegelman rejects any metalanguage of symbolization and meaning, whether it be the official language of Holocaust memorials or the discourse that insists on thinking of Auschwitz as a telos of modernity. The approach to Holocaust history is sought in an intensely personal, experiential dimension that finds expression in a whole variety of

different media and genres. The prerequisite for any mimetic approximation (of the artist/reader/viewer) is the liberation from the rituals of
mourning and of guilt. Thus it is not so much the threat of forgetting as
the surfeit of memory[28] that is the problem addressed by such newer work.
How to get past the official memorial culture? How to avoid the trappings
of the culture industry while operating within it? How to represent that
which one knows only through representations and from an ever-growing
historical distance? All this requires new narrative and figurative strategies
including irony, shock, black humor, even cynicism, much of it present in
Spiegelman's work and constitutive of what I have called mimetic approximation. *Bilderverbot* is simply no longer an issue since it has itself become
part of official strategies of symbolic memorializing. This very fact may
mark the historical distance between Adorno (whose "after Auschwitz"
chronotope, with its insistence on the prohibition of images and the barbarism of culture, has a definite apocalyptic ring to it) and these younger
postmodernist writers and artists to whom the prohibition of images must
appear like Holocaust theology. But if, on the other hand, Adorno's notion of mimesis can help us understand such newer artistic practices and
their effects in a broader frame, then there may be reasons to suspect that
Adorno's rigorously modernist reflection itself blocked out representational possibilities inherent in that mimetic dimension. In its hybrid fold-
ing of a complex and multilayered narration into the mass cultural genre,
Spiegelman's image-text makes a good case against a dogmatic privileging
of modernist techniques of estrangement and negation, for it demonstrates
how estrangement and affective mimesis are not mutually exclusive but
can actually reinforce each other.

Finally, there is a weaker, less apocalyptic reading of Adorno's "after
Auschwitz" statements. Such a reading would emphasize Adorno's historical critique of that attempt to resurrect German culture after the catastrophe, that attempt to find redemption and consolation through classical
cultural traditions—Lessing's *Nathan, der Weise* as proof of German "tolerance" of the Jews, Goethe's *Iphigenie* as proof of German classical hu-
manism, German poetry, music, and so forth: "Healing through quotation," as Klaus Scherpe has called it.[29] The spirit of such a critique of an
official German post-Auschwitz culture is one that Adorno shares with the
newer generation of artists in many countries today, all of whom try to
work against contemporary versions of official Holocaust culture the di-

mensions of which Adorno could not even have imagined during his lifetime. There is another sentence of Adorno's, less frequently quoted, but perhaps more pertinent today than the famous statement: "To write poetry after Auschwitz is barbaric." This sentence continues to haunt all contemporary attempts to write the Holocaust: "Even the most extreme consciousness of doom threatens to degenerate into idle chatter."[30] Only works that avoid that danger will stand. But the strategies of how to avoid such degeneration into idle chatter in artistic representations cannot be written in stone.

9

Rewritings and New Beginnings: W. G. Sebald and the
Literature on the Air War

The political divide of 1989 inevitably raises the question how German literature has been affected after the fall of the Wall. The question "what remains," articulated by Christa Wolf in her controversial book *Was bleibt*, published in 1990, inevitably raises the other question of what has changed on the German literary scene in the 1990s. But it also compels us to reconsider the whole course of postwar German literature since 1945 in the light of unification. Change inevitably points to erosions, to forgetting, even to endings as it points, sometimes, to new beginnings. The phrase *Was bleibt* (what remains) carries all these connotations: fading residue, stable and shifting canon, and new departure.

We all remember the longing for new beginnings at the time of unification. The feuilletons conjured up new beginnings in literature, film, the visual arts, and intellectual life. Today such memories are just that—memories. Ten years after those intense and exhilarating times, it seems to make more sense to ask whether this desire for always new beginnings isn't as much of a problem as the parallel desire for the stability of a canon. After all, the longing for new departures has long since been the flip side of the desire for that which remains, one of the permanent fixtures, it seems, of the culture of modernity since Romanticism. And yet, in postfascist Germany the desire for new beginnings has always taken on very specific connotations.

Clearly, political unification in 1990 did not produce a vibrant upsurge in literature and the arts, nor was it ever plausible to assume that the return to national unity would produce anything surprisingly new in literature and the arts to begin with. Only at great peril to each have politics and aesthetics ever marched in lockstep, and today the nation no longer provides the primary nurturing and securing frame for literature that it did provide at an earlier time. As a result, some have begun to lament the decline of German literature generally, thus engaging in a discourse of cultural loss that has its own deep history. Others will happily forget literature and celebrate the new media instead. I will do neither but will focus on the desire itself for repeated new beginnings, a peculiar German repetition compulsion of the postfascist decades that is only now coming into fuller view.

More than a decade after the fall of the Berlin Wall and the collapse of the Soviet Union, we may indeed want to consider how these events may force us to reassess the field of post-1945 German literature and culture from today's perspective. Such reassessment was at stake in the Christa Wolf debate of 1990, with its critical broadsides not just against Wolf but against the Gruppe 47 and the cherished notion of a *littérature engagée*.[1] Since then the attempt to recode the literary and historical past in service to the present has witnessed further discursive eruptions, such as the one triggered by Botho Strauss with his essay "Anschwellender Bocksgesang" in 1992, or by Martin Walser's 1998 speech in the Frankfurt Paulskirche and by the claims he made for the innocence of his generation's Nazi childhood in the novel *Ein springender Brunnen*.[2] But every one of these debates has remained mired in scandal and in the cultural politics of the day. The German desire for new beginnings itself, however, has not received much sustained attention, even though the historical watershed of 1989–90 now offers interesting points of comparison with other key moments of the postwar period.

In this essay, I first suggest some of the problems any such broader reassessment of postwar German literature will encounter in the context of postunification cultural politics. Second, I draw on W. G. Sebald's book-length essay *Luftkrieg und Literatur* (*The Air War and Literature*, 1999), which lends itself particularly well to a focus on the obsession with endings and new beginnings, that peculiar structure of repetition in postwar German literature and culture at large.

To focus on the repetition entailed in new beginnings is not to deny literary evolution and change since 1945. Rather, it is to counter an approach to literary history that operates with stable and bounded territorial entities and follows the orderly chronology of decades and generations, thus blocking from view the multiple rewritings and cross-textual relations that are part and parcel of the larger historical frame of postwar German culture.[3] Ultimately, my reading of Sebald is meant as a case study of how the rewriting of a literary and historical past since 1945 is tied to a structure of national memory that stretches across generations and decades.

Reconfiguring Literary History: Restoration vs. 1968

First, then, some comments on the issue of reconfiguring postwar German literature. Although the history of German literature, East and West, has been written and appears fairly stable in its general outlines, the interpretation of that history remains very much contested. Unification has triggered a war of interpretations that is energized by several forms of mythmaking and memory politics regarding not just the 1990s but the early postwar decades themselves in relation to the present. This is, of course, not only a question of literary history.

The fact that 1989–90 represents such a convenient marker of closure to postwar literary developments should be considered a problem rather than the cure for literary history. For we now have an all too convenient and teleological block narrative: German literature from 1945 to 1990, from capitulation/liberation via the divided nation to national unification. Of course, there was the earlier discussion of one, two, or even four German literatures: literature written in German; East German literature and German literature written in the West; West German, East German, Austrian, and Swiss literatures. There also are well-established subdivisions by temporal markers such as 1945–49, 1949–59/61 or –68, 1968–89. But one such marker has become a major bone of contention in Germany in recent years: 1968. The public debate about the legacies of 1968, no doubt exacerbated by the proximity of the thirtieth anniversary of 1968 in 1998 and, in 1999, the fiftieth anniversary of the founding of the Federal Republic itself, has had its literary-historical resonances with the ambitious 1998 anniversary exhibit at the national literature archive in Marbach, entitled *Protest! Literatur um 1968*.[4]

Briefly, the issue is this. The 1990s have witnessed an intensified attempt to give a more positive spin to the early postwar years and the Adenauer chancellorship. This view challenges the left-liberal consensus of the previous decades that the 1950s were a period of restoration. The reevaluation of the early years of the Federal Republic of Germany (FRG), ultimately in the name of a retroactive "normalization," tries to clear the Adenauer years from the foul odor of the restoration reproach. But its hidden agenda is to deny that 1968 played a major role in the cultural, literary, and political development of postwar German democracy. There is nothing wrong with dismantling certain myths about 1968, but not if the only result is the replacement of one myth by another.

Symptomatic of this tendency is a slim book of literary criticism published in 1997 and edited by Walter Erhart and Dirk Niefanger, entitled *Zwei Wendezeiten: Blicke auf die deutsche Literatur 1945 und 1989.*[5] The lead essay by Helmut Kiesel, who also contributed a major essay to the catalogue of the Marbach show on the literature of 1968, proposes that the concept of a restoration period in the FRG was purely a literary invention, rather than a historical reality.[6] Kiesel laments the lingering effect of this concept among those literary historians who remain reticent about wholly accepting the harmonious message about the achievements of the Adenauer period. Completely illogically, Kiesel then mobilizes critical authors of the 1950s (Wolfgang Koeppen, Günter Eich, Hans Werner Richter), some of the sharpest oppositional voices of the restoration, as proof that there cannot have been a real restoration to begin with; for otherwise these authors would not have been able to write what they wrote. This is a kind of argumentative *Gleichschaltung* (synchronization) of literature and politics if ever there was one: as if a restorative regime and its radical critique could not have existed side by side.

The argument is bizarre—the presence of a strong critique of the restoration, say, in Koeppen's novel *Das Treibhaus*, is used as proof that that which is criticized did not exist. The bone of contention here obviously lies in the word *restoration*. I would like to make three points about this argument:

1. One can easily agree that certain 1960s Marxist forms of the restoration thesis that saw the FRG as a protofascist state deserve to be criticized; but that was done long ago by Ralf Dahrendorf and other political scientists of differing persuasions, and even by Hans Werner Richter himself. Such agreement does not require that we abandon the notion of restoration altogether as a description of the 1950s.[7] Clearly, to use the term *restoration* is not to suggest that the fascist state was restored in West Germany. It *is* to

imply that the culture of the Federal Republic, especially but not only in the private domain of family life and the *Stammtisch*, was still pervaded by a tradition of conservative, authoritarian, and nationalist thinking that had its roots in the Wilhelmian period and had certainly been part of the National Socialist cultural synthesis. We should also remember that most of the literary production of the 1950s (e.g., the literature of suspicion of ideology [*Literatur des Ideologieverdachts*]) and even of that of the 1960s (e.g., language experimentalism) was not dependent on such Left political critiques to begin with. By blaming the restoration thesis on writers and literary critics, Kiesel makes an ideological rather than a literary argument. But why now again and why with this vehemence? What is at stake here for the writing of postwar literary history?

2. This latest revisionism regarding the 1950s, which is also widespread in the media, has two purposes: it is aimed at undercutting any claims that "1968" (shorthand for the late 1960s, its events and ideals) represented a kind of historical watershed in West German culture and politics comparable to the *Wende* (turn) of 1989–90. The restoration thesis, after all, was the basis for the emphatic claim that 1968 was a key turning point in German literary history. Further, by eliminating 1968 as a constitutive part of the postwar narrative of German culture and democracy, the revisionist view succeeds in giving a foundationalist account of the old FRG according to which the grounds for German democracy were laid in the late 1940s by what it calls a "fundamental modernization" (*durchgreifende Modernisierung*), and the telos of development was reached in the second "turning point" (*Wendezeit*) of 1989–90, with unification.[8] The myth of 1968 that grounded what I have elsewhere called the left-liberal consensus of the 1970s and 1980s has thus been replaced with the conservative myth of "two turning-points" (*zwei Wendezeiten*), which are held to ground the legitimacy and cultural authenticity of a democratic Germany.[9]

3. Minimizing the importance of 1968 today has yet another function. It was the 1960s that first brought the Holocaust openly into public debate in the FRG: texts by Frisch, Hochhuth, Weiss, Walser, Kluge, Hildesheimer, and many others come to mind. While the antifascism of the 1960s Left may in the end have been as problematic and helpless as the "helpless antifascism" of the older generation the Left was attacking, it was the 1960s that first brought the Nazi past back to German consciousness and public debate in a way that the reparation policies of the Adenauer

government in the 1950s had been designed to avoid. However critical we may want to be today of the specific ways in which writers in the 1960s represented the Holocaust (I'm thinking here of Peter Handke's attack performance at the meeting of the Gruppe 47 in Princeton in 1966 or of the problematic instrumentalization of the Holocaust for a critique of capitalism in Peter Weiss and others), the public memory debate in Germany received its first major impetus precisely in the context of a protest movement that had lasting effects on literary developments thereafter. This may not be the way in which the actors of 1968, measured by their own intentions, wanted to be remembered either literarily or politically, but it certainly makes the 1960s an inalienable part of German postwar culture.[10]

At the same time, we do need the critique of the 1960s, both of the last decade of the Gruppe 47 *and* of the various radical solutions proposed to overcome the crisis of German *belles lettres*, but this critique needs to be articulated in ways that go beyond attempts to create a proper national narrative by simply erasing the 1960s as an irrelevant aberration from the course of German history and literature.[11] Perhaps it is a blessing that the Federal Republic of Germany actually lacks a strong foundational narrative. The continuing quarrel about 1945, 1968, and 1990 may point to a political strength, not a weakness. The more important differentiation of the present from the past may, after all, not be achieved with reference to any of these dates, but rather with a view to the overriding reality of living post-Auschwitz. As Dan Diner recently suggested, "Auschwitz" has become something like a civic religion in Germany, and, for better or for worse, it may by now have become a foundational myth of the new Europe.

Turning Points

The end of World War II was a turning point, a *Wendezeit* for all Germans. The end of the war, the defeat of the Nazi state, and life in the ruins of the bombed cities provided Germans with a common body of experience, even though conditions varied somewhat under different occupations. The year 1989–90 was again a turning point for the nation, but it was experienced by East Germans, whose everyday lives had to confront wrenching adjustments and changes, in a radically different manner from West Germans, for whom nothing much seemed to change at the material level of everyday life. In the following, I discuss the matter of turning points as they affect the West German perspective. My argument, especially as regards 1989–90 (but also 1945 and 1968), would have to be made differently for the German Democratic Republic (GDR) and post-GDR, where the obsession with new beginnings was equally salient but was coded differently from the West.

My suggestion here is to take the notion of a new beginning as a key myth of postwar German literature and trace it over the postwar decades. My purpose is not to invent a kind of bildungsroman of the German republic, which is what the "*zwei Wendezeiten*" approach intends. Rather, it is to insist on the continued and continuing reinscription of that which comes before the "post" (postwar, post-Shoah, postunification). The word *reinscription* points to a historical condition and to a literary operation, as well as to a set of generational and literary memories that affect writers and writing in complex and different ways; yet this should *not* result in the moral demand that the writer be *das Gewissen der Nation* (the conscience of the nation), or, as we might put it today, the witness and carrier of national memory.

In retrospective, the insistence on new beginnings—on *Neuanfänge, Nullpunkte, tabula rasa, Wendepunkte,* and the like—appears a peculiarly German obsession that links such seemingly different imaginaries as those of 1945, 1968, and 1989. The multiplicity of new beginnings results not only from historical events and constellations but also from the absence of the kind of foundational narrative that Gaullist France created around the Resistance and that the East German state produced with its dogma of antifascism. The paradox of the West German case is that every emphatic claim about a new beginning can also be read as a repetition.

For some, there may be something counterintuitive about an argument that reads 1968 as a repetition by reversal of 1945, a year that, in the minds of the sixty-eighters, had failed to provide a clean break with Fascism. From this perspective, 1968 would be the renewed attempt to achieve a degree zero of literature and culture, a radically fresh start beyond "bourgeois *belles lettres*," and thus a repetition of the *Nullpunkt* of 1945 with a different cast of characters and different goals. Separation from the past, at any rate, was the primary goal in both cases.

Perhaps less counterintuitive after the debates of the 1990s is the suggestion that 1989–90 can be read as a repetition by reversal of 1968, a call yet again for a new literature, this time one embodying a purer aesthetic beyond the allegedly dominant *Gesinnungsästhetik* (aesthetics of conviction) of the previous period, as articulated influentially in the early 1990s by Karl Heinz Bohrer and in the feuilletons of the *FAZ* and *Die Zeit.*[12] In all three cases, however, the emphatic demand for the new very soon proved to have been illusory at best.

Counterintuitive or not, there are several methodological advantages in focusing on the notion of repetition as a template through which to look at postwar German literature at these crucial junctures. Such a focus avoids metanarratives of evolution and political teleology. It avoids locating the phantasms of originary foundations and authenticity in the immediate postwar period or at other turning points in German history. And most important, it allows us to link together authors who would otherwise remain separated by criteria of chronology, decades, generations, or writing strategies. As I show later, Sebald's memory texts revolve crucially around such repetitions.

Obviously, the focus on turning points is intensely invested in notions of endings and new beginnings. Ever since the 1960s, we have come to see the idea that 1945 was a literary *Nullpunkt* as a delusion or a self-serving ideological ploy. And 1968 never was the radical literary rupture it pretended to be. More important, recent literary theory has given us concepts that allow us to understand all literature—indeed, all writing—as constitutively intertextual, rhetorical, woven of traces and supplements, insertions and erasures, filiations and affiliations that would make the very idea of a *Nullpunkt* obsolete to begin with. And yet the myth of *Nullpunkt,* the *Wende,* the new beginning, keeps coming back in different guises: in the *Nullpunkt* and the literature of the ruins (*Trümmerliteratur*) after 1945; in the much-touted death of literature and the emergence of operative writing, documentary, and reportage in the 1960s; in the farewell of 1990 to the literature of the FRG; and in Frank Schirrmacher's thinly veiled attack on the Gruppe 47 twenty and some years after the group's expiration, combined with his call for "a new way of telling time, in story-telling as well": in short, for a newer and purer aesthetic.[13]

Why this repetitive obsession, which is clearly fueled by much more than simply the avant-gardist claim for the new? There are specific historical and ideological explanations for each one of these "turning points." But there is perhaps another dimension, one not so easily captured: a dimension that has something to do with the double-edged desire simultaneously to remember and to avoid the past, a habitus of memory politics that is more than simple forgetting or repression. The question then arises: Can we read the intensity of the desire for new beginnings as a repetition compulsion rooted in traumatic historical experience? And if so, what constitutes trauma for the Germans and how can we read the repetitive mise-en-scène of the traumatic experience, if that is what it is, without denying historical difference in the various successive repetitions and without getting stuck in the psychoanalytic dead end of poststructuralist trauma theory?[14] Such questions, of course, cannot be answered in general but only through a focus on specific texts and discourses. For when we ask about postwar German trauma, things immediately get difficult. Clearly this trauma is made up of various layers—the feeling of the humiliation of total defeat, which is not erased by emphasizing that capitulation was also liberation; the deep guilt feelings about the Holocaust, itself not a German trauma but rather the trauma of its victims, which as such blocks the desired normalization; the experience of expulsion from the East and the experience of the bombardment of German cities, both of which have been used either to constitute the German as victim in an *Aufrechnungsdiskurs*, a compensatory discourse of moral equity (look how *we* suffered), or as a cathartic argument that retribution was justified (serves us right!) with permanent implications for national identity and statehood.

My hypothesis is that at its deepest level the German discourse of turning points from 1945 on can be read as a symptom of such multilayered traumatic experiences, which always leave something unresolved and in need of further articulation.[15] After every turn, it seems, the past returns only to generate the desire for the next turn. At the same time, this repetitive dialectic between memory and forgetting has not locked German public culture in the structure of frozen melancholy. Since every repetition differs from the last, there is movement in public memory, a movement not toward resolution or even redemption, but toward acknowledgment and recognition.

Writing and Rewriting the Air War

Let me turn now to W. G. Sebald's *Luftkrieg und Literatur*, a slim but important book that is centrally concerned with the experience of saturation bombings as a specifically German trauma, and with what it alleges to have been the psychic repression of that trauma in postwar Germany. As a critical essay about the few literary texts treating the subject since the mid-1940s, Sebald's book lends itself well to a discussion of the structure of repetition that haunts the sequence 1945–1968–1989/90.

We have many studies about representations of the Holocaust in German literature and film since the 1940s, but the topic of the air war against German cities has received only scant attention. The *Trümmer-literatur* of the 1950s, a "literature of the ruins" often written by war veterans returning from the front, focused on life in the ruins after the war, not on the experience of the bombings themselves. And then there emerged a political taboo, pertinent for critical intellectuals especially in the 1960s. To speak about the air war seemed inescapably tied to the discourse of German victimization and thus to a relativization or denial of the Holocaust. Today this taboo has lost its force. There simply is no good reason not to include the experience of the bombings in a discussion of the early postwar imaginary in Germany. The many reviews that attacked *Luftkrieg und Literatur* as yet another attempt to exculpate the Germans as victims were simply off the mark. Sebald is not an *Aufrechner*, is not tallying moral equity, and cannot be read according to this old paradigm.

However, I do not intend to follow Sebald's own explicit and highly problematic intention of documenting yet another German repression, this time not the inability to mourn but a refusal to remember. Sebald accuses German writers of repressing the past in having failed to represent the destruction of German cities, just as Germans in general have been said to repress the Holocaust. In its accusatory tone, the book lapses into the discourse of *Abwicklung*, of a settling with the past, that was so prominent in the debate of 1990 about Wolf's *Was bleibt*, and the reader begins to wonder what may be at stake for Sebald, given the vehemence of his accusation.

At the same time, Sebald's repression hypothesis may be the least persuasive aspect of his argument, and it must share the fate of any and all repression hypotheses. Rather than generating silence, as we have learned from Foucault, repression generates discourse. The scarcity of literary texts about the bombings may have to be explained differently, and it certainly contrasts with the fact that there always was a lot of *talk* about the bombings in postwar Germany. After all, it was that kind of ubiquitous talk, familiar to all who grew up in West Germany in the 1950s, that produced the taboo on discussing the air war among liberals and leftists in the first place. Such discussion was perhaps more prevalent in the private than in the public sphere, but it functioned powerfully in bolstering the war generation's claims to having been victimized and the attempt to minimize responsibility. *Both* the Holocaust and the strategic bombings were very much part of the postwar social imaginary in Germany from the very beginning, and neither could be had without the other.

What is interesting in Sebald's book is not the phenomenon he purports to establish as yet another repression—the absence of literary texts about the bombings.[16] It is rather the way he reads the texts about the bombings that do actually exist: primarily Erich Nossack's *Der Untergang* (1948), Alexander Kluge's *Der Angriff auf Halberstadt* (1977), and, more marginally, Hubert Fichte's *Detlevs Imitationen "Grünspan"* (1971). Surprisingly, Sebald never acknowledges the widespread theoretical discourse of the 1990s about trauma, repetition, and the aporias of representation, although his awareness of the issue pervades the narratives of *Die Ausgewanderten*, which was written in 1992.[17] I would like to suggest that Sebald's *Luftkrieg und Literatur* is itself a repetition, a rewriting of those earlier texts about the experience of strategic bombing; and, second, that it is closely related—in its deep structure, its conceptual framework, and its language (though not in its narrative complexity)—to the narrative stance of *Die Ausgewanderten* itself. The mediating link between these two very different texts, between the historical critical essay and the four stories, which some consider Sebald's most powerful literary work, is the memory problematic of the second generation, of Germans who were born and grew up after the war. Nossack, Kluge, and Fichte experienced the bombings. Sebald did not.

Memory and rewriting, then, are the issue. Nossack's narrative about the devastating attack on Hamburg in the summer of 1943 has always been read as symptomatic of its time—the time of the last phase of the war and of the new beginning it made necessary. Fichte's incorporation of the same bombing of Hamburg into his novel was motivated by the twenty-fifth anniversary of that bombing, in 1968. The pertinent passages in *Detlevs Imitationen "Grünspan"* are clearly marked in their writing strategy as a countertext to Nossack's. This was clearly a rewriting by a writer of the next generation who had witnessed the bombing as a child rather than as an adult and whose literary sensibilities were those of a later generation. Nossack belonged to the generation Sigrid Weigel has recently described as the "secret first generation," those who made up the core of the Gruppe 47 and who had started their writing careers during or even before the war.[18] Both Fichte (born in 1935) and Kluge (born in 1932), on the other hand, are generationally located between the "secret first generation" and the second generation proper, those like Sebald (born in 1944) who do not have early childhood memories of the Third Reich.

Kluge's *Angriff auf Halberstadt*, written in the early 1970s and published in 1977 in the volume *Neue Geschichten*, was part of Kluge's analytic writings about war, but it also was an attempt to approach an inerasable childhood memory via documentation and fictionalization.[19] Actually, Fichte's and Kluge's texts both used a mix of fiction and documentation, albeit in significantly different ways, at a time when the documentary mode was still very much in vogue. But in the 1960s, the first major phase of the public Holocaust memory discourse in Germany, documentation was focused primarily on the crimes of the Nazis and their collaborators, not on the war experience of the German civilian population.[20] Thus neither Fichte's nor Kluge's text had much resonance at the time—certainly less than Sebald's *Luftkrieg und Literatur* did in the late 1990s. And Nossack was all but forgotten by the late 1960s.

Luftkrieg und Literatur performs a kind of secondary traumatic repetition after the *Wende* of 1989–90, just as Kluge's and Fichte's texts had enacted symptomatic repetitions after the critical times of 1968, and Nossack's right after the bombing of Hamburg in the summer of 1943. With Nossack, with Kluge and Fichte, and then with Sebald himself, we have four texts about the bombardments, each of which is loosely related to one of the three major turning points in postwar German history: 1945, 1968, and 1989–90. Although each repetition has to be read on its own terms, it is clear that they represent three distinct generational moments: traumatization through direct experience with Nossack as adult and with Fichte and Kluge as children, transgenerational traumatization absent the experience itself in the case of Sebald.[21]

For unmistakably, Sebald's essay is not just an analysis of those earlier writers' work but a hidden rewriting of both Nossack's and Kluge's texts. Thus Sebald's treatment of memory and his incorporation of photographs into all his texts is clearly reminiscent of Kluge's text/image strategies in *Neue Geschichten*. In both Kluge's and Sebald's writing, the frequent lack of captions to pictures leaves the reader unsure of the status of photographed images and their relation to the text. At the same time, Sebald's own narrative style and use of language in a text like *Die Ausgewanderten* rely on slower-paced writing strategies of the nineteenth century (reminiscent especially of Adalbert Stifter), strategies that clash in estranging ways with the psychic catastrophes that make up the content of the stories.[22] Here the distance from Kluge's modernist strategy of fast-paced discourse montage is most evident. And yet, the stories of *Die Ausgewanderten* could also be described with the title of another collection of Kluge's stories: *Lernprozesse mit tödlichem Ausgang* (*Learning Processes with Lethal Consequences*).

In the idea of a natural history of destruction (*Naturgeschichte der Zerstörung*) that grounds his imagination, however, Sebald's conceptual framework includes elements of a traditional metaphysics of nature lacking in Kluge but overbearingly present in Nossack's narrative. At the same time, Sebald tries to gain a certain distance from Nossack's expressionist ruminations about war as a revolt of nature. Instead he codes his "natural history of destruction" with the help of Walter Benjamin's apocalyptic imagery of the angel of history, quoted extensively at the end of the book's second major chapter, which concludes the Zurich lectures of 1997 from which the book was reworked.[23] But I doubt whether he really does more here than provide a respectable pedigree to what remains a metaphysics of nature in his own writing.

These are only some of the most obvious aspects of an intense intertextuality that binds together these three texts on the air war by Nossack, Kluge, and Sebald, an intertextuality on which Sebald himself never reflects in his text. It is as if his main thesis about the failure of the older generation of writers, which would presumably include both Nossack and Kluge, were intended to hide his dependence on their approach to the topic. But it may not be a question of intention at all. Instead, this may well be Sebald's blind spot. His reductive attack on German writers of an earlier generation and on their failure to represent and commemorate the air war becomes a kind of compensation—compensation, I would suggest, for the fact that Sebald, a member of the first post–forty-five generation, born in the Allgäu in 1944 far away from the stream of bombers, has no access to the experience or memory of the air war except through these earlier texts that he is compelled to rewrite, in a kind of literary version of transgenerational traumatization.

At the same time, his rewriting points powerfully to the fact that there was always something unresolved in German memories of the war. Ironically, the feuilleton critiques of Sebald that reiterated the old leftist taboo against making the air war part of public discourse tended thus to confirm the repression hypothesis in another sense.[24] What may be subliminally at stake here is not the psychic repression of the air war by those who experienced it but its political repression by the second generation, Sebald's own. This may well explain the vehemence of his accusations.

But Sebald's text is not only dependent on these earlier writers' texts in that he traces their complex documentary modes of writing. His political stance is curiously reminiscent of the 1960s repression reproach itself, which was then concerned with the repression of the Holocaust rather than with memories of the air war. But just as the sixty-eighters claimed that "bourgeois literature" was unable to come to terms with the Third Reich, Sebald accuses that same generation of older writers for not even having tried to recall its consequences. It is yet another repetition from yet another angle.

Posttraumatic New Beginnings

All survivors of traumatic experiences face the difficult task of new beginnings. But the tension between traumatic symptom and new beginning will necessarily remain unresolved, generating ever new attempts at resolution. It is far too simple to believe, as Sebald evidently does, that the presence of a great war and postwar epos could have prevented collective damage to what he calls (problematically) "das Seelenleben der deutschen Nation" (the spiritual life of the German nation): the great writer of the air war not as the conscience of the nation à la Böll or Grass, but as the nation's shrink.[25] After all, we know that every posttraumatic new beginning bears the traces of traumatic repetition, even though increasing temporal and generational distance from the original experience may alter the discursive structure of the posttraumatic symptom.

Historians have described how the urban populations of postwar Germany reacted with numbness and apathy to the experience of loss and destruction only to throw themselves into the frenetic activity of reconstruction and to embrace consumerism as a way to forget. Such strategies of compensation can also be found in the texts on the air war themselves and in the ways they insist on new beginnings. Sebald's own analysis of Nossack and Kluge could have told him how traumatic experience and the drive toward a posttraumatic new life remain indissolubly tied to each other and defy easy resolution. Ultimately this is also true of Sebald's own text.

Nossack, Kluge, and Sebald all emphasize the weight of history and the pull of its gravity. But they differ in the ways they imagine new beginnings. In Nossack, traumatic experience is transcended in an existentialist discourse of freedom from history, even a feeling of happiness (*Glücksgefühl*) about the total loss of the past that Nossack codes as fairy tale:[26]

There was once a man whom no mother had borne. A fist pushed him naked into the world, and a voice called: See how you manage. Then he opened his eyes and did not know what to do with what was around him. And he dared not look behind him, for behind him was nothing but fire.[27]

The overdetermination of this writing by allusion to the fairy tale, to Sartrean existentialism, and to the Bible points to the posttraumatic strategy of symptomatic avoidance and the delusion of a new beginning—one of the key dialectics of postwar existentialism in West Germany. It also allows Nossack to deal with diffuse feelings of guilt.[28] And it explains the attractiveness of the *Nullpunkt* thesis and of the notion of rebirth in the postwar years. Thus Nossack's text ends with a birthing metaphor: "We had to get out through a hole, and in front of the hole the flames were leaping to and fro. . . . So I wrapped a wet blanket around my head and crawled out. Then we were through."[29] *Der Untergang*, which offers a sober and factual reportage in many of its parts, cannot do without such metaphysical transcendence and transfiguration, which also manifests itself in the repeated motif of nature rising up against itself, as if the issue were nature rather than history and politics.[30]

Kluge's text, in its entirety more sober and matter of fact than Nossack's, avoids Nossack's expressionist imagery of myth, nature, and notions of a universal human destiny. It is anti-expressionist and anti-existentialist to the core. The first-person author/narrator appears only once, and laconically, in the introduction: "The form of the impact of a high-explosive bomb is easily remembered. It consists in a shortening. I was there when, on April 8, 1945, one such impacted at a distance of 10 meters."[31] Kluge remains thoroughly and self-consciously focused on the multiplicity of discourses—experiential, journalistic, bureaucratic, sociological, photographic, and statistical—that make up the discursive totality of strategic bombing. What

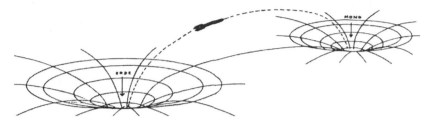

FIGURE 9.1 The flight from the earth to the moon. An attempt to sketch the relations of gravity. Oskar Negt and Alexander Kluge, *Geschichte und Eigensinn* (Frankfurt am Main: Zweitausendundeins, 1981), 789.

holds this text montage together is the distinction between what Kluge calls the strategy from above (the military planners, the planes, the bombs) from a strategy from below: the futile attempts of the bombed to escape and to survive. Strategic bombing appears inexorable, the historically inevitable result of large-scale industrial progress and capitalist development, and Kluge's text ends with the comment of an interviewee: "Once you've reached a certain point of atrocity, it doesn't matter who's done it: it should only stop."[32] If saturation bombings of civilian populations are seen as the logical result of capitalist development rather than as the result of specific political calculations, then there does not seem to be a place for any new beginning short of the end of capitalism itself. But Kluge's critical Marxism, nurtured by Adorno's social theory, refuses such easy utopias.

However, in *Geschichte und Eigensinn,* a book coauthored with Oskar Negt, Kluge reflects again on his spatial categories of above and below as a way of envisioning relational positions in history (*Stellung im Geschichtsverhältnis*). Here, with the aid of an astronautic metaphor, he imagines a moment or point of total freedom from history, where the gravity of historical relations is overcome and where above and below are momentarily reversed.[33]

In space flight, the moment of release from planetary gravity on the way from one planet to another is called the "abaric point" (*abarischer Punkt*). While this abaric point, a point or moment of freedom, is always only imagined or thought, it could be a point of release from the past, of release from the pull of traumatic repetition. And although Kluge seems far removed from the air war in this discussion, I am struck by his choice of visual image. Both the rocket and the representation of gravitational pull as funnels of gravity (*Gravitationstrichter*)—and who would not think here of the German word for bomb craters, *Bombentrichter*—pull the reader back to the relations of history and the air war that frame this abstract discussion of the abaric point to begin with. And yet, unlike Nossack, Kluge has no illusions about achieving any abaric point in the sphere of history or experience. This represents an unattainable horizon. In his text on the air war, the weight of historical relations remains dominant and insuperable.

Sebald does not articulate a "feeling of happiness" à la Nossack, nor do we find the equivalent of an abaric point in his writings. *Die Ausgewanderten* is relentlessly melancholy and caught in a web of traumatic memories. However, a moment of freedom may occur in the contradictory experience of readers lured and nurtured by Sebald's deceptively traditional and beautiful prose, despite the melancholy content of the narratives. A kind of poetic freedom emerges precisely from Sebald's relentless explorations of individual life histories caught in the slow death of exile. But this is not the autonomy of the aesthetic mobilized in the early 1990s by Karl Heinz Bohrer and others against a *littérature engagée* and the aesthetics of conviction. Nor do these stories aestheticize the individual catastrophes they depict. Aesthetically and historically precise, Sebald's investigations of the past in *Die Ausgewanderten* permit the reader to envision the catastrophes of the twentieth century without sentimentality and without ideology and abstraction. Sebald's is a unique voice on the literary scene, the voice of a latecomer (*Nachgeborener*) in a new sense, of one who rewrites the texts of the past and who remembers the concrete texture of the lives lost. Thus it is not surprising that there is no strong notion of a new beginning in Sebald's writings, which are so aware of the palimpsestic nature of all *écriture*. Words such as *Neuanfang* or *Wende* don't seem to be part of his vocabulary. But then Sebald himself points to a major difference between himself and the three older writers he discusses: "Born in May of 1944 in the Alpine region of Allgäu, I am one of those who remained as good as untouched by the catastrophe that was then taking place in the German Reich."[34] Yet he acknowledges that the catastrophe left traces of memory that he tried to articulate in some of his other works. Thus in *Vertigo* (*Schwindel. Gefühle*), we read:

. . . in nearly every weekly news reel we saw the mountains of rubble in places like Berlin and Hamburg, which for a long time I did not associate with the destruction wrought in the closing years of the war, knowing nothing of it, but considered them a natural condition of all larger cities.[35]

Given this personal history, it becomes clear why Sebald's own understanding of the air war was centrally shaped by the earlier literary texts. But it is the notion of ruins as a natural condition of all bigger cities that points back to Sebald's own childhood memories and accounts for his difference from Kluge. At stake here is Sebald's move from history and politics to the notion of a natural history of destruction.

Interestingly, Sebald's *Luftkrieg und Literatur* is itself a rewrite of an earlier essay entitled "Between History and Natural History: An Essay on the Literary Description of Total Destruction with Notes on Kasack, Nossack and Kluge."[36] The difference between this text of 1982 and the book of 1999 is telling. If in 1982 Sebald located himself on the threshold between history and natural history, in the more recent work he clearly comes down on the side of the latter. Symptomatic is his rereading of Kluge at the end of the second chapter of *Luftkrieg und Literatur*, where he draws on Marx's and Kluge's analyses of industrial history to ask a rhetorical question about destruction:

The history of industry as the open book of human thinking and feeling—can the materialist theory of knowledge, or any and every theory of knowledge be maintained in the face of such destruction, or is this not the irrefutable warning that the catastrophes developing under our noses and then breaking out with seeming abruptness anticipate, in a sort of experiment, the point at which we shall sink back from our allegedly autonomous sphere of history into the history of nature?[37]

Of course, this is a rhetorical question, and the suggested answer of total despair is not one that Kluge would have embraced. The text then ends with the familiar passage from Walter Benjamin's thesis about the angel of history, but the messianic dimension inherent in Benjamin's thought, even at its most desperate and pessimistic, no longer finds a place in Sebald. It is as if history itself had been bombed into oblivion.

By contrast, Sebald's discussion of Kluge in the text of 1982 still suggests the possibility of a learning process "that is not doomed in advance to a lethal outcome."[38] Kluge's work is seen here as critical labor on the regeneration of collective memory, and this didactic project, for which Sebald shows unmitigated sympathy, is said to keep the author from yielding to the temptation "to interpret the most recent historical developments simply as natural history."[39] By the 1990s, Sebald himself has yielded to that temptation. Not only is there no new beginning, but there does not seem to be a future. Sebald's text of 1999 ends in a loop back to Hitler's 1940 fantasy of a total demolition of London and to the German bombing of Stalingrad in August 1942—a closed circuit of destruction with another suggestive loop back to Kluge's writings about Stalingrad.

In sum, then, Sebald—who unlike Nossack, Kluge, and Fichte did not experience the bombings, but grew up in the shadow of "the catastrophe"—gives us not so much an analysis as a reinscription of the trauma by means of quotation. As such, this is the secondary trauma of the "second" generation, always already mediated through literature, images, and representations, and perhaps on that account not susceptible to imagining new beginnings. At the same time, the discourse of a natural history of destruction remains too closely tied to metaphysics and to the apocalyptic philosophy of history so prominent in the German tradition and recoded in a variety of ways in the postwar period. It was exactly this type of discourse that Kluge and Fichte countered in their narrative practice of discourse montage, irony, and satire. I'm not sure whether the return of this type of discourse in Sebald says something about the pathology of German memory culture of the 1990s at large or whether it is only the imaginary of one expatriate writer working from the margins of the German literary scene.

However one may answer such a question, Sebald's critical and literary texts point powerfully to one of the fundamental conditions of postwar German literature. Like the public culture from which postwar German literature emerged and that it shaped in turn, this literature lives off repetitions, reinscriptions, and rewritings that make any historical account of postwar literary developments as a stable progression through the decades inherently problematic. Equally problematic is the attempt to short-circuit the relation between literature and politics along the lines of the thesis of "two turning-points." The relationship of literature to politics and history is not captured by the notion of political turns or new beginnings, nor is it adequately discussed in the notion of an autonomy of the aesthetic sphere, an idea that has had a surprising rebirth in the 1990s. Sebald's own work of storytelling—especially in *Die Ausgewanderten*, but also, though differ-

ently, in his most recent novel, *Austerlitz*[40]—gains some of its power precisely because it remains outside of such reductive alternatives.

Sebald's storytelling maintains a strong link among narrative, document, and history, and it codes that link aesthetically in terms of literary
memory. In the context of the often overbearing memory culture of the
1990s, it may not always escape the danger of mannerism, a danger that af-
fects all self-consciously palimpsestic writing projects. Maybe there is
something of a new beginning in this literary high-wire act. But we certainly would not want to call it a *Wende*.

10

Twin Memories: Afterimages of Nine/Eleven

In a culture as obsessed with memory such as ours, it is not surprising that the debate about how to commemorate the attack on the twin towers began to stir soon after the traumatic shock. Spontaneous memorials and "missing" notices replete with vital data and photographs sprang up everywhere in downtown Manhattan—in subway stations, on storefronts, at bus stops. Flowers at many of these sites indicated that there was not much hope to find any of the missing. A whole part of Manhattan had been turned into a cemetery, but a cemetery without identifiable bodies and without graves—a death zone in which the work of cleanup and removal went on day and night.

The ruins were still smoldering with underground fires when the architects and developers came forth, emphasizing the need to rebuild fast and big, possibly even bigger than before: no ruins allowed in the American imagination. At the same time, a consensus has emerged that there must be some permanent memorial to the tragic loss of life that traumatized New York. Any memorial will also have to commemorate what may turn out to have been a major turning point in world history, not just the history of the city or the history of the United States. How can one reconcile the desire to rebuild a prime site of real estate with the need to commemorate the dead, and with the challenge to memorialize a historical event? Anybody who knows about the frustrating debates and unsatisfactory "solutions" concerning the commemoration of historical trauma and criminal terror elsewhere, even decades after the commemorated events, must fear the worst. The Oklahoma memorial with its 168 empty chairs symbolizing the number of the victims reminds one of the theater of the absurd, and Peter Eisenman's Holocaust memorial in Berlin, once it is built, has the potential of becoming a monumental memory sore rather than the space for historical reflection that was intended. The issue here is not the imaginative ability or inability of artists, architects, and designers, but rather the objective problems of representing and memorializing traumatic events in built space, especially if that space is a death zone in living memory. And there is an added problem for the memorians in New York: How does one imagine a monument to what was already a monument in the first place—a monument to corporate modernism? No surprise that some suggested rebuilding an exact replica of the twin towers. The idea is as absurd as it is intriguing in its logic: the rebuilt twin towers as a monument to forgetting, an erasure of history, an emblem of global capital in a different sense from that of the terrorist imaginary.

The real debate about "ground zero," however, has moved on. Discussions about how to memorialize 9/11 are gathering steam, though they are not yet fully public in New York at a time when the media are still so busy with the war front. No doubt, the memorial debate will soon grow by leaps and bounds, driven by the narcissism of victimization and accelerated by its convergence with the short-term time frame of developers and city politicians. Given such objective pressures, it seems quixotic to suggest that it is not yet the time to have this debate. Considering New York's recent record of urban planning and building, slowing down seems unlikely unless forced by the economic downturn. Neither rampant nationalism nor the raw emotions of injury and anger have ever produced persuasive monuments in urban space. This, then, may be a good moment to reflect on something else. For me, the theme of memory and the twin towers conjures up images of events in the past rather than the future of memory—events that in my own imagination have attached themselves closely to the collapse of the twin towers.

In the rare moments of reflection not tied to daily news events in the fall of 2001, I've been surprised at how persistently the afterimage of the twin towers hovers in my mind. Clearly they carry symbolic meaning more forcefully than the partially destroyed Pentagon. But this symbolic meaning is not that of the terror of globalization and hegemonic power, as the blow-back theorists argue and as it seems to function in the terrorists' own imaginary. No single and not even a twin corporate tower could ever represent the nature of global capital, nor could its destruction equal the collapse of capital. This is infantile symbolism. For a New Yorker by choice, it is a different symbolism that counts. The image of the twin towers simply represented home in the metropolis. Often, you first saw them approaching New York from the air. Year after year, you saw them in the distance driving back home from the airports in Queens, Brooklyn, or New Jersey. Unwieldy and ugly as they were, they anchored the island's skyline in the south. Their monumental size crowded out other landmarks. Monumentality itself is at the core of their afterimage and its effects.

Thinking about the buildings as buildings and as symbols, memories of two other images and events crowd in, superimposing themselves on the television sequences of the unfolding disaster. When I saw the twin towers collapse on television on the morning of 9/11—despite shock over the unfathomable loss of human life and a fleeting fear about a potential nuclear device on board the planes—I was instantly reminded of images showing the controlled implosion in 1972 of another icon of modern architecture: the Pruitt Igoe Housing project in St. Louis, designed by the same architect who built the World Trade Center, Minoru Yamasaki—a haunted architect, if ever there was one. Pruitt-Igoe became an icon only through its very destruction, images of which have widely circulated both on television and in architecture books. That implosion of thirty years ago has been described time and again as a symbolic marker for the end of urban modernism and the beginning of postmodernism in architecture. The twin towers, however, were completed in 1973 and 1976, respectively, after that supposed historical break, that is, and they were built in the spirit of the classical modernist skyscraper and its vertical sublime. In 1972, it was supposedly the end of urban modernism. Now we hear talk of the end of the skyscraper, coupled with renewed fears about the end of urban life and public space. Early suggestions to protect New York by closing Times Square to traffic, transforming it into a tourist mall, were joined by such ideas as limiting access to railroad terminals and to public parks—all in the name of creating defensible space. None of that will fly. Sure, some will go live in Celebration, Florida, and New York may have to go through another bad period of economic downturn, rising unemployment, and urban decay, not just as a result of 9/11, but as a consequence of the mega-delusions and speculative frenzy of the 1990s. But

New York will not end up lying flat. Neither modernism nor the skyscraper are dead. The key issue will rather be how to rethink both in relation to metropolitan public and civic space, in relation to business culture, and in relation to governmental responsibility and civic politics. The implosion of 1972 did not generate much in the way of urban renaissance. Only time will tell whether the collapse of the twin towers will generate imaginative alternatives for an urban restructuring of the southern tip of Manhattan.

The other more recent image that sadly attaches itself to the disappearance of the twin towers in clouds of smoke and debris opens up another, perhaps more political dimension. What I have in mind is the dynamiting of the two Bamiyan Buddha statues near the Hindu Kush mountains in central Afghanistan. In the spring of 2001, after having massacred many of the Shia minority Hazaras living in the Bamiyan valley, the Taliban destroyed these two sublime statues which had inspired awe and wonder for centuries on the silk road, itself one of the earlier emblems of transcontinental, if not global, trade at another crossroads of the world in another time. The Islamic Pashtuns and other Islamic Afghan tribes had lived for hundreds of years with these millennial statues carved out of a massive sandstone cliff. The Bamiyan statues stood as an emblem of cultural syncretism and religious tolerance. Suddenly, almost five years into Taliban rule, they were declared blasphemous, and a seemingly disproportionate effort was mounted by the Taliban to destroy them. Why?

Threats to the statues were first articulated by Taliban military leaders in 1998 after the American missile strike against one of Osama bin Laden's training camps. But it was only in late February 2001 that Mullah Muhammad Omar issued a *fatwa* calling for the destruction of all figurative statues in Afghanistan in line with Islamic law. The Buddha statues were dynamited in mid-March. In the meantime, the international media had been flush with appeals to the Taliban and with criticisms of their cultural barbarism. Parallels were drawn with other state-sponsored iconoclasms such as China's cultural revolution, the Nazi destruction of Jewish artifacts in the Third Reich, and the Serbian destruction of Muslim cultural sites in Bosnia. Kofi Annan and UNESCO, governments of many Asian countries with large Buddhist populations as well as major international museum figures intervened in a futile effort to save the statues. At the time, there was speculation in the press that the Taliban acted out of defiance—defiance of the international community which still refused to recognize the Taliban government as legitimate. Links were also established in the press with the illegal antiquities trade in which the Taliban were complicit, secretly selling off Afghanistan's cultural heritage under the veil of self-righteous religious iconoclasm.

But as we know more now about the extremely close relationship, if not dependence of Mullah Omar on Al Qaeda and Osama bin Laden since the mid-1990s, it is difficult not to think about the relationship between the attack on the two sublime Bamiyan statues and the subsequent attack on the differently sublime twin towers. It is as if the dynamiting and collapse of the two statues last spring had been a carefully staged prologue to the attack on New York, symbolic actions both, intended to whip up support for bin Laden's apocalyptic Islamism in the Muslim world. The parallels are obvious. Two figures each, one taller than the other, like brothers; both invested in the aesthetic of the sublime; but not the terrorizing sublime which makes the spectator feel small and overwhelmed, for both allowed a view from the top, from the top of the World Trade Center as from the top of the Buddha's cave. In both cases, in the paranoid aggressive world of the Taliban and Al Qaeda, the aesthetics of the sublime represents only the demonic power of the other—the other religion, the other way of life, the infidel. But we can now surmise that the links go beyond symbolism.

The documented influence of Saudi Wahhabism on the Pakistani *madrasas* and on the Taliban makes it entirely plausible to suggest that the Wahhabist presence in Afghanistan that had grown during the Soviet occupation played a key role in the destruction of the Buddhas, invaluable monuments to the art and civilization of Afghanistan and the world. And Wahhabi presence in Kandahar points to Al Qaeda and bin Laden. Whether or not bin Laden took an active part in formulating Mullah Omar's *fatwa*, it is not difficult to imagine bin Laden and his co-conspirators enjoying the international uproar about the attack on the Buddhas as it played out over weeks in the world media while they were anticipating the deadly attack on the twins, then already at an advanced stage of planning.

Of course, there are differences. The iconoclasm of the Taliban follows the logic of a local theocracy and the religious policing of its subject population. The iconoclasm of bin Laden and his co-conspirators, on the other hand, stages a deadly world-media event in order to deal a blow to that very modernity of which bin Laden himself is a product, both in his own socialization as a construction engineer and in his political trajectory toward terrorism since the 1980s. But bin Laden's iconoclasm goes hand in hand with a very modern iconolatry: bin Laden posing as prophet on the tapes broadcast to the Muslim world via Al Jazeera, bin Laden in front of his cave, bin Laden shooting off a submachine gun surrounded by his followers, bin Laden's image on posters and T-shirts wherever his message resonates. The iconic visibility of bin Laden contrasts curiously with the invisibility of Mullah Omar, whom we have only known from a grainy, unfocused photograph.

Now that we have seen the latest bin Laden tape and that we have read the utterly vacuous and pompous transcript of his and his companions' allegedly prophetic dreams of flying and fantasies of apocalyptic destruction, devoid of politics and interspersed with sanctimonious incantations, it is easy to see what the dynamiting of the Bamiyan Buddhas has in common with the attack on the twin towers. This is not the banality of evil Hannah Arendt once analyzed as key to the bureaucratic mindset of Adolf Eichmann. It is rather the banality of a religious zealotry, which has caused so much suffering and destruction over the centuries whenever it has allied itself successfully with state power. What is at stake here is not the moral struggle of good vs. evil, a discourse that itself remains deeply embedded in self-righteous religious thinking. Demonizing the terrorists only reiterates what they themselves do in their hatred for the infidel. Politicized religious zealotry, whether of Islam, Christianity, Judaism, or any other religion, is not the other of modernity, but its very product. At stake therefore is the political struggle to combat religious zealotry in all its forms, with the goal of preventing it from infiltrating or capturing state power wherever it may threaten to do so. To win that struggle, strategies other than military ones are needed. Questions of political power and economic devastation need to be addressed, as well as deficits of meaning, histories of humiliation and injustice, the downside of globalization which is mostly forgotten when one looks at the world from a 1990s Western perspective only. In the meantime, the twin memories keep haunting me. And if I look closely at images of the now empty cave that held the larger of the two very human Buddha statues, I take comfort in the fact that in the back of the cave, the human outline of the destroyed statue is still visible, if only barely: another afterimage, supporting another memory that lingers.

Notes

CHAPTER I. PRESENT PASTS

1. Both the title of this essay and the notion of "present futures" are indebted to the seminal work of Reinhart Koselleck, *Futures Past* (Boston: MIT Press, 1985).

2. Of course, an emphatic notion of "present futures" still operates in the neo-liberal imaginings of financial and electronic globalization, a version of the former, largely discredited modernization paradigm updated for the post–Cold War world.

3. Paradigmatically in Fred Jameson's classic essay "Postmodernism or the Cultural Logic of Late Capitalism," *New Left Review* 146 (July–August 1984): 53–92.

4. David Harvey, *The Condition of Postmodernity* (Oxford: Basil Blackwell, 1989).

5. See Arjun Appadurai, *Modernity at Large: Cultural Dimensions of Globalization* (Minneapolis and London: University of Minnesota Press, 1998), esp. chapter 4, and most recently the special issue *Alter/Native Modernities* of *Public Culture* 27 (1999).

6. On the complex mix of present futures and present pasts, cf. Andreas Huyssen, "The Search for Tradition" and "Mapping the Postmodern," in *After the Great Divide: Modernism, Mass Culture, Postmodernism* (Bloomington: Indiana University Press, 1986), 160–78, 179–221.

7. See Charles S. Maier, *The Unmasterable Past* (Cambridge, Mass.: Harvard University Press, 1988); *New German Critique* 44 (Spring/Summer 1988), special issue on the *Historikerstreit*; and *New German Critique* 52 (Winter 1991), special issue on German reunification.

8. Cf. Anson Rabinbach, "From Explosion to Erosion: Holocaust Memorialization in America since Bitburg," *History and Memory* 9:1/2 (Fall 1997): 226–55.

9. Of course, the use of Holocaust memory as a prism for the events in Rwanda is highly problematic since it cannot acknowledge the specific problems arising within a postcolonial memory politics. But that was never the issue in Western media accounts. On memory politics in various parts of Africa, cf.

Richard Werbner, ed., *Memory and the Postcolony: African Anthropology and the Critique of Power* (London and New York: Zed Books, 1998).

10. This view was first articulated by Horkheimer and Adorno in their *Dialectic of Enlightenment*, and it was taken up again and reformulated by Lyotard and others in the 1980s. On the centrality of the Holocaust for Horkheimer and Adorno's work, see Anson Rabinbach, *In the Shadow of Catastrophe: German Intellectuals Between Apocalypse and Enlightenment* (Berkeley: University of California Press, 1997).

11. Gerhard Schulze, *Die Erlebnisgesellschaft: Kultursoziologie der Gegenwart* (Frankfurt and New York: Campus, 1992). The term *Erlebnisgesellschaft*, literally "society of experience," is hard to translate. It refers to a society that privileges intense but superficial experiences oriented toward instant happiness in the present and quick consumption of goods, cultural events, and mass-marketed lifestyles. Schulze's is an empirical sociological study of contemporary German society that avoids the restrictive parameters both of Bourdieu's class paradigm and of Benjamin's philosophically inflected opposition of "Erlebnis" and "Erfahrung" as an opposition between fleeting surface and authentic depth experience.

12. On Chile see Nelly Richard, *Residuos y metáforas: Ensayos de critica cultural sobre el Chile de la transición* (Santiago: Editorial Cuarto Propio, 1998); on Argentina see Rita Arditti, *Searching for Life: The Grandmothers of the Plaza de Mayo and the Disappeared Children of Argentina* (Berkeley and Los Angeles: University of California Press, 1999).

13. My use of the notion of "imagined memory" is indebted to Arjun Appadurai's discussion of "imagined nostalgia" in his *Modernity at Large*, 77f. The notion is problematic to the extent that all memory is imagined, and yet it allows us to distinguish memories grounded in lived experience from memories pillaged from the archive and mass-marketed for fast consumption.

14. On these issues cf. Miriam Hansen, "*Schindler's List* Is Not *Shoah*: The Second Commandment, Popular Modernism, and Public Memory," *Critical Inquiry* 22 (Winter 1996): 292–312. Also the essay "Of Mice and Mimesis: Reading Spiegelman with Adorno," in this book.

15. Dennis Cass, "Sacrebleu! The Jazz Era Is Up for Sale: Gift Merchandisers Take License with History," *Harper's Magazine* (December 1997): 70–71.

16. Hermann Lübbe, *Zeit-Verhältnisse: Zur Kulturphilosophie des Fortschritts* (Graz and Vienna: Verlag Styria, 1983). For a more extended critique of Lübbe's model, see my "Escape from Amnesia: The Museum as Mass Medium," in *Twilight Memories: Marking Time in a Culture of Amnesia* (London and New York: Routledge, 1995), 13–36.

17. Quoted from the *New York Times* (February 12, 1998).

18. The term is Charles S. Maier's. See his essay "A Surfeit of Memory? Reflections on History, Melancholy, and Denial," *History and Memory* 5 (1992): 136–51.

CHAPTER 2. MONUMENTAL SEDUCTION

1. On the broader implications of the recent memory boom, see my *Twilight Memories: Marking Time in a Culture of Amnesia* (New York and London: Routledge, 1995).

2. Quoted from *Badisches Tagblatt*, July 24, 1995.

3. Robert Musil, "Nachlaß zu Lebzeiten," in *Gesammelte Werke*, vol. 2, ed. by Adolf Frisé (Reinbek: Rowohlt, 1978), 506–9.

4. Axel Hecht, "Editorial," *art spezial* (July 1995): 3.

5. Letter to Uhlig, September 20, 1850, in *Richard Wagner's Letters to His Dresden Friends*, trans. by J. S. Shellock (New York: Scribner and Welford, 1890), 69.

6. Thomas Mann, "Suffering and Greatness of Richard Wagner," *Essays of Three Decades*, trans. H. T. Lowe-Porter (New York: Knopf, 1971), 315.

7. Walter Benjamin, "Moscow Diary," in *October* 35 (Winter 1985): 65.

8. Michel Foucault, Preface to Gilles Deleuze, Félix Guattari, *Anti-Oedipus: Capitalism and Schizophrenia* (Minneapolis: University of Minnesota Press, 1983), xiii.

9. Denis Hollier, *Against Architecture: The Writings of Georges Bataille* (Cambridge, Mass., and London: MIT Press, 1989).

10. The published English translation is insufficient. It only speaks of the "world-historical task." *Richard Wagner's Prose Works*, trans. by William Ashton Ellis, vol. 1: *The Art work of the Future* (New York: Broude Brothers, 1966), 130.

11. Wagner, *Art-work of the Future*, 162.

12. Friedrich Nietzsche, "Nachgelassene Fragmente," in *Sämtliche Werke*, vol. 8, ed. by Giorgio Colli and Mazzino Montinari (Munich: Deutscher Taschenbuch Verlag, 1980), 501 (my trans.).

13. Richard Wagner, "Art and Revolution," in *Richard Wagner's Prose Works*, vol. 1, 35.

14. Wagner, *Art-work of the Future*, 104f. Translation corrected.

15. Richard Wagner, "Opera and Drama," in *Richard Wagner's Prose Works*, vol. 2, 189 (translation corrected).

16. Inexplicably, only part of the passage is translated in Wagner, *Richard Wagner's Letters to, Dresden Friends*, 140. For the original German, consult Wagner, *Sämtliche Briefe, IV: Briefe der Jahre 1851–1852* (Leipzig, 1979), 176.

17. Mann, "Suffering and Greatness of Richard Wagner," 376.

18. *Cosima Wagner's Diaries, II (1878–1883)*, edited and annotated by Martin Gregor-Dellin and Dietrich Mack, trans. by Geoffrey Skelton (New York and London: Harcourt Brace Jovanovich, 1980), 561.

19. Letter to Uhlig of October 22, 1850, in *Richard Wagner's Letters to Dresden Friends*, 85.

20. "Nine Points on Monumentality," in Siegfried Giedeon, Fernand Léger,

and José Luis Sert, *Architecture, You and Me: The Diary of a Development* (Cambridge, Mass.: Harvard University Press, 1958), 48–51.

CHAPTER 3. THE VOIDS OF BERLIN

1. Michael Kimmelman, "That Flashing Crazy Quilt of Signs? It's Art," *New York Times* (Dec. 31, 1996): 1.

2. Karl Scheffler, *Berlin—Ein Stadtschicksal* (Berlin: Fannei und Walz, 1989 reprint), 219.

3. Ernst Bloch, *Erbschaft dieser Zeit* (Frankfurt am Main: Suhrkamp, 1973), 212–28. Of course, Bloch's phrasing "Funktionen im Hohlraum" (literally, functions in a hollow space) suggests a bounded void that after all is appropriate whenever one discusses a void in a spatial or temporal sense.

4. See Bertolt Brecht, "Against Georg Lukács," trans. Stuart Hood, in Ernst Bloch et al., *Aesthetics and Politics* (London: Verso, 1977), 68–85.

5. As quoted by Francesca Rogier, "Growing Pains: From the Opening of the Wall to the Wrapping of the Reichstag," *assemblage* 29 (1996): 50.

6. Peter Schneider, *The Wall Jumper: A Berlin Story* (Chicago: University of Chicago Press, 1998).

7. Bernard Tschumi, *Event Cities* (Cambridge, Mass.: MIT Press, 1994), 367.

8. Saskia Sassen, *The Global City: New York, London, Tokyo* (Princeton, N.J.: Princeton University Press, 1991).

9. Some of the key contributions to the debate about critical reconstruction are collected in *Einfach schwierig: Eine deutsche Architekturdebatte*, ed. Gert Kähler (Braunschweig: Vieweg, 1995).

10. As quoted in Dagmar Richter, "Spazieren in Berlin," *assemblage* 29 (1996): 80.

11. Hans Stimmann, "Conclusion: From Building Boom to Building Type," in Annegret Burg, *Downtown Berlin: Building the Metropolitan Mix/Berlin Mitte: Die Entstehung einer urbanen Architektur*, ed. Hans Stimmann, trans. Ingrid Taylor, Christian Caryl, and Robin Benson (Berlin, 1995).

12. "Daniel Libeskind mit Daniel Libeskind: Potsdamer Platz" (1992), in Daniel Libeskind, *Radix—Matrix: Architekturen und Schriften* (Munich and New York: Prestel, 1994), 149.

13. For a gentle, though to me ultimately unpersuasive, critique of Libeskind's void as being too determined by history, meaning, and experience, see Jacques Derrida, "Jacques Derrida zu 'Between the Lines'," in Libeskind, *Radix—Matrix*, 115–17.

14. This is implied by Derrida, for whom a void that represents is no longer a proper void.

15. A competition in 1995 with a total of 527 entries ended in a public outcry over the winning entry, a slanted concrete slab the size of two football fields with millions of victim names carved in stone. Even Helmut Kohl did not like it, though surely for the wrong reasons. The debate continued until Peter Eisenman's

proposal was accepted several years later, but at the time of this writing this monument to the murdered Jews of Europe has not yet been erected.

16. I am only talking here about the building as architecture. Its museal and curatorial functions are still too much in flux for us to comment with any degree of certainty about the ways in which the exhibition spaces will be used or even who will have ultimate curatorial control over the expansion space.

CHAPTER 5. FEAR OF MICE

1. On Disney in Germany, see J. P. Storm and M. Dressler, *Im Reiche der Mickey Mouse: Walt Disney in Deutschland 1927–1945* (Berlin: Henschel, 1991).

2. Eric Rentschler, *The Ministry of Illusion* (Cambridge, Mass.: Harvard University Press, 1996).

3. On the Adorno/Benjamin Disney debate, see Miriam Hansen, "Of Mice and Ducks: Benjamin and Adorno on Disney," *South Atlantic Quarterly* 92:1 (Winter 1993): 27–61. For another detailed Marxist critique of Disney, see Ariel Dorfman and Armand Mattelart, *How to Read Donald Duck: Imperialist Ideology in the Disney Comic*, trans. and introduction by David Kunzle (New York: International General, 1975).

4. Saskia Sassen and Frank Roost, "The City: Strategic Site for the Global Entertainment Industry" (unpublished paper).

5. Cf. the essays in this book "The Voids of Berlin" and the later "After the War," which discuss the Potsdamer Platz development at different stages in the mid- and late 1990s.

6. Michael Kimmelman, "That Flashing Crazy Quilt of Signs? It's Art," *New York Times* (Dec. 31, 1996): 1.

7. At the time of this writing (1997), one office tower at the northeast corner of Broadway and Forty-second Street is already being built and a second one has been approved. Two more are under consideration.

8. Joan Ockman, "From Sin City to Sign City: The Transformation of Times Square," in Pellegrino D'Acierno, ed., *(In)visible Cities: From the Postmodern Metropolis to the Cities of the Future* (New York: Monacelli, forthcoming 2003). See also Marshall Berman, "Women and the Metamorphoses of Times Square," *Dissent* (Fall 2001): 71–82.

CHAPTER 6. MEMORY SITES IN AN EXPANDED FIELD

1. Rosalind Krauss, "Sculpture in the Expanded Field," *October* 8 (Spring 1979), reprinted in Krauss, *The Originality of the Avantgarde and Other Modernist Myths* (Cambridge, Mass.: MIT Press, 1985), 276–90.

2. Pierre Nora, *Realms of Memory: The Construction of the French Past, Vol. 1, Conflicts and Divisions* (New York: Columbia University Press, 1996).

3. Marguerite Feitlowitz, *A Lexicon of Terror: Argentina and the Legacies of Tor-*

ture (Oxford: Oxford University Press, 1998). See also Rita Arditti, *Searching for Life: The Grandmothers of the Plaza de Mayo and the Disappeared Children of Argentina* (Berkeley: University of California Press, 1999).

4. For an account of the difficulties that arise from the comparison of the Holocaust with other traumatic historical events, see the title essay in this book, "Present Pasts."

5. Jan Assmann, "Collective Memory and Cultural Identity," *New German Critique* 65 (Spring/Summer 1995): 125–34.

6. For an excellent account of the institutional and political background of the park project, see Graciela Silvestri, "El arte en los límites de la representación," *Punto de vista* 68 (December 2000): 18–24.

7. I will not discuss here the plan to clutter this evocative landscaping project with a series of sculptures that will inevitably wreak havoc with the architectural concept. That concept relies on the simplicity of landscape form and on the visual resonance between the monument itself and the La Plata River. The addition of sculptures of whatever kind along the river pathway will inevitably destroy the effect so carefully calibrated by the architects. The already mentioned article by Graciela Silvestri gives a cogent critique of the sculpture competition and its negative effect on the park.

8. Derek Walcott, *Omeros* (New York: Farrar, Straus and Giroux, 1990), 204.

9. I say this recognizing that the Argentinean dirty war claimed a relatively high number of Jewish victims and that one of the most powerful documentaries about the American war in Vietnam was called "The War At Home." But the deadly fate of the *desaparecidos* was not primarily caused by a racial ideology, nor did the American war at home ever come close to the state terror unleashed in Argentina, Uruguay, or Chile at the time.

CHAPTER 8. OF MICE AND MIMESIS

1. Anson Rabinbach, *In the Shadow of Catastrophe: German Intellectuals between Apocalypse and Enlightenment* (Berkeley: University of California Press, 1997).

2. Central here is the chapter entitled "Elements of Antisemitism" in Horkheimer and Adorno's classic work *Dialectic of Enlightenment*, originally published in 1947, English translation by John Cumming (New York: Continuum, 1982).

3. As is to be expected, the discussion of signification, hieroglyphs, language, and image is pre-Saussurean, presemiotic in the strict sense. It remains indebted to Benjamin on the one hand, and through Benjamin also to a nineteenth-century tradition of German language philosophy. But it is precisely the non-Saussurean nature of this thought that allows the notion of mimesis to emerge in powerful ways.

4. See Gertrud Koch, "Mimesis und Bilderverbot in Adorno's Ästhetik," in Koch, *Die Einstellung ist die Einstellung* (Frankfurt am Main: Suhrkamp, 1992).

5. See Josef Früchtl, *Mimesis: Konstellation eines Zentralbegriffs bei Adorno* (Würzburg: Könighausen & Neumann, 1986); Karla L. Schultz, *Mimesis on the Move: Theodor W. Adorno's Concept of Imitation* (Bern: Peter Lang, 1990); Gunter Gebauer and Christoph Wulf, *Mimesis: Kultur, Kunst, Gesellschaft* (Reinbek: Rowohlt, 1992), esp. 374–422; Martin Jay, "Mimesis and Mimetology: Adorno and Lacoue-Labarthe," in Jay, *Cultural Semantics* (Amherst: University of Massachusetts Press, 1998), 120–37.

6. Theodor W. Adorno, *Minima Moralia: Reflections from a Damaged Life*, trans. E.F.N. Jephcott (London: Verso, 1974), 154.

7. Theodor W. Adorno, Review of Roger Caillois, *La Mante religieuse*, *Zeitschrift für Sozialforschung* 7 (1938): 410–11. See also Adorno's letter to Benjamin of September 22, 1937, and Benjamin's response in his letter of October 2, 1937, in *Theodor W. Adorno—Walter Benjamin: Briefwechsel 1928–1940*, ed. by Henri Lonitz (Frankfurt am Main: Suhrkamp, 1994), 276–78, 286.

8. The literature on representing the Holocaust is by now legion. One of the richest and still influential collections of essays is Saul Friedlander, ed., *Probing the Limits of Representation: Nazism and the "Final Solution"* (Cambridge, Mass.: Harvard University Press, 1992). Most recently Dominick LaCapra, *History and Memory after Auschwitz* (Ithaca and London: Cornell University Press, 1998).

9. Art Spiegelman, *Maus I: A Survivor's Tale. My Father Bleeds History* (New York: Pantheon, 1986), and *Maus II: A Survivor's Tale and Here My Troubles Began* (New York: Pantheon, 1991). Page references will be given in the text.

The following publications were extremely helpful in preparing this essay. I acknowledge them summarily since my concern is a theoretical proposition rather than a new and differentiated reading of the text per se. Joseph Witek, *Comic Books as History* (Jackson, Miss., and London: University Press of Mississippi, 1989); Andrea Liss, "Trespassing Through Shadows. History, Mourning, and Photography in Representations of Holocaust Memory," *Framework* 4:1 (1991): 29–41; Marianne Hirsch, "Family Pictures. *Maus*, Mourning, and Post-Memory," *Discourse* 15:2 (Winter 1992–93): 3–29; Miles Orvell, "Writing Posthistorically. *Krazy Kat, Maus,* and the Contemporary Fiction Cartoon," *American Literary History* 4:1 (Spring 1992): 110–28; Rick Iadonisi, "Bleeding History and Owning His [Father's] Story: *Maus* and Collaborative Autobiography," *CEA Critic: An Official Journal of the College English Association* 57:1 (Fall 1994): 41–55; Michael Rothberg, "We Were Talking Jewish". Art Spiegelman's *Maus* as 'Holocaust' Production," *Contemporary Literature* 35:4 (Winter 1994): 661–87; Edward A. Shannon, "'It's No More to Speak'. Genre, the Insufficiency of Language, and the Improbability of Definition in Art Spiegelman's *Maus*," *Mid-Atlantic Almanach* 4 (1995): 4–17; Alison Landsberg, "Toward a Radical Politics of Empathy," *New German Critique* 71 (Spring/Summer 1997): 63–86. And most recently Dominick LaCapra, "'Twas Night before Christmas: Art Spiegelman's *Maus*," in LaCapra, *History and Memory after Auschwitz* (Ithaca and London: Cornell University Press, 1998); James

Young, "The Holocaust as Vicarious Past: Art Spiegelman's *Maus* and the After-images of History," *Critical Inquiry* 24:3 (Spring 1998): 666–99.

10. For a discussion of the worst offenders, see Michael Rothberg, "After Adorno: Culture in the Wake of Catastrophe," *New German Critique* 72 (Fall 1997): 45–82.

11. The paradox is that when Adorno accused poetry after Auschwitz of barbarism, he deeply suspected the apologetic temptation of a poetic and aesthetic tradition, whereas much of the recent poststructuralist discourse of the sublime in relation to Holocaust representations does exactly what Adorno feared: it pulls the genocide into the realm of epistemology and aesthetics, instrumentalizing it for a late modernist aesthetic of nonrepresentability. A very good documentation and discussion of notions of the sublime can be found in Christine Pries, ed., *Das Erhabene: Zwischen Grenzerfahrung und Größenwahn* (Weinheim: VCH Acta Humaniora, 1989).

12. Paradigmatically in Shoshana Felman's much discussed essay "The Return of the Voice: Claude Lanzmann's *Shoah*," in Shoshana Felman and Dori Laub, *Testimony: Crises of Witnessing in Literature, Psychoanalysis, and History* (New York: Routledge, 1992), 204–83. For a convincing critique of Felman's work, see Dominick LaCapra, *Representing the Holocaust: History, Theory, Trauma* (Ithaca and London: Cornell University Press, 1994), as well as LaCapra, *History and Memory After Auschwitz* (Ithaca and London: Cornell University Press, 1998). The latter volume also contains a well-documented essay on Spiegelman's *Maus* that includes a critical discussion of much of the literature on this work.

13. This argument has been made very forcefully and persuasively in Miriam Hansen, "*Schindler's List* Is Not *Shoah*: The Second Commandment, Popular Modernism, and Public Memory," *Critical Inquiry* 22 (Winter 1996):292–312. For the earlier debate on the TV series *Holocaust*, a similar argument can be found in Andreas Huyssen, "The Politics of Identification: *Holocaust* and West German Drama," in *After the Great Divide: Modernism, Mass Culture, Postmodernism* (Bloomington: Indiana University Press, 1986), 94–114.

14. These were central topoi in the German debate about Holocaust memory. See the special issue on the *Historikerstreit*, *New German Critique* 44 (Spring/Summer 1988), as well as Charles S. Maier, *The Unmasterable Past: History, Holocaust, and German National Identity* (Cambridge, Mass.: Harvard University Press, 1988).

15. Cf. the two-page prologue initiating volume one dated Rego Park, N.Y.C., 1958, when Art is only ten years old, or the photo of his dead brother Richieu that overshadowed his childhood, but is later used at the beginning of volume two to dedicate this part of the work to Richieu and to Nadja, Art Spiegelman's daughter.

16. The category of working through has been most thoroughly explored for this context by Dominick LaCapra, *Representing the Holocaust: History, Theory, Trauma* (Ithaca and London: Cornell University Press, 1994). LaCapra bases his approach on Freud, and he acknowledges that there cannot be a rigorous and

strict separation between acting out and working through for trauma victims. Although I feel certain affinities to LaCapra's general approach, I prefer not to engage the psychoanalytic vocabulary. While the psychoanalytic approach is certainly pertinent to the analysis of survivor trauma, it does have serious limitations when it comes to artistic representations of the Holocaust and their effect on public memory. The notion of "mimetic approximation" that I try to develop through my reading of *Maus* tries to account for that difference.

17. Significantly, the prologue to volume one that shows Artie roller-skating and hurting himself is also dated 1958, and when just a few pages and many years later Artie asks his father to tell his life's story, he is looking at a picture of his mother and is saying: "I want to hear it. Start with Mom . . . " (I:12).

18. With this insight and so much more, my reading of *Maus* is indebted to Marianne Hirsch's incisive essay "Family Pictures: *Maus*, Mourning, and Post-Memory," *Discourse* 15:2 (Winter 1992–93): 3–29. Reprinted in Hirsch, *Family Frames: Photography, Narrative, and Postmemory* (Cambridge, Mass.: Harvard University Press, 1997). Cf. also M. Hirsch, "Projected Memory: Holocaust Photographs in Personal and Public Fantasy," in Mieke Bal, Jonathan Crewe, and Leo Spitzer, eds., *Acts of Memory: Cultural Recall in the Present* (Hanover and London: University Press of New England, 1999), 3–23.

19. See note 6.

20. See Homi K. Bhabha, "Of Mimicry and Man: The Ambivalence of Colonial Discourse," in Bhabha, *The Location of Culture* (New York and London: Routledge, 1994), 86.

21. Interview conducted by Gary Groth, "Art Spiegelman and Françoise Mouly," in Gary Groth and Robert Fiore, eds., *The New Comics* (New York: Berkley, 1988), 190–91.

22. These are the terms Horkheimer and Adorno use in the first chapter of the *Dialectic of Enlightenment*, where they discuss the irremediable splitting of linguistic sign and image. Horkheimer and Adorno, *Dialectic of Enlightenment*, 17–18.

23. Miriam Hansen, "Mass Culture as Hieroglyphic Writing: Adorno, Derrida, Kracauer," *New German Critique* 56 (Spring/Summer 1992): 43–75. Gertrud Koch, "Mimesis und Bilderverbot in Adorno's Ästhetik," in Koch, *Die Einstellung ist die Einstellung* (Frankfurt am Main: Suhrkamp, 1992), 16–29.

24. Horkheimer and Adorno, *Dialectic of Enlightenment*, 24. In German: "Gerettet wird das Recht des Bildes in der treuen Durchführung seines Verbots," Theodor W. Adorno, *Gesammelte Schriften* 3 (Frankfurt am Main: Suhrkamp, 1983), 40.

25. Quoted in Joshua Brown's review of *Maus I* in *Oral History Review* 16 (1988): 103–4.

26. "A Conversation with Art Spiegelman. With John Hockenberry," *Talk of the Nation*, National Public Radio, February 20, 1992.

27. An observation I owe to Gertrud Koch.

28. The term is Charles S. Maier's. See his essay "A Surfeit of Memory? Reflections on History, Melancholy, and Denial," *History and Memory* 5 (1992): 136–51.

29. Klaus R. Scherpe, ed., *In Deutschland unterwegs 1945–48* (Stuttgart: Reclam, 1982).

30. Theodor Adorno, *Prisms* (Cambridge, Mass.: MIT Press, 1981), 34.

CHAPTER 9. REWRITINGS AND NEW BEGINNINGS

1. See Andreas Huyssen, "After the Wall: The Failure of German Intellectuals," in *Twilight Memories: Marking Time in a Culture of Amnesia* (London and New York: Routledge, 1995), 37–66. For a full documentation of the debate, see Karl Deiritz and Hannes Krauss, eds., *Der deutsch-deutsche Literaturstreit* (Hamburg: Luchterhand, 1991); Thomas Anz, ed., *"Es geht nicht um Christa Wolf": Der Literaturstreit im vereinten Deutschland* (Munich: Edition Spangenberg, 1991).

2. For the debate about Strauss, see the collection of essays in *Weimarer Beiträge* 40 (2/1994). Martin Walser's speech is published as Martin Walser, "Erfahrungen beim Verfassen einer Sonntagsrede," in *Friedenspreis des deutschen Buchhandels. Ansprachen aus Anlaß der Verleihung* (Frankfurt am Main: Suhrkamp, 1998), 37–51. For a subtle and relentlessly critical view of Walser's controversial speech and its relation to *Ein springender Brunnen,* see Amir Eshel, "Vom einsamen Gewissen: Die Walser-Debatte und der Ort des Nationalsozialismus im Selbstbild der Berliner Republik," *Deutsche Vierteljahrsschrift* 74 (2000): 333–60.

3. On the relation of postwar German literature to an earlier modernism, see Klaus R. Scherpe, *Die rekonstruierte Moderne: Studien zur deutschen Literatur nach 1945* (Cologne: Böhlau, 1992). On the problematic literary and generational claims of a Nullpunkt in 1945, see especially Hans Dieter Schäfer, "Zur Periodisierung der deutschen Literatur seit 1930," in *Literaturmagazin 7: Nachkriegsliteratur* (Reinbek: Rowohlt, 1977), 95–115. For a recent reassessment of the *Stunde Null* by historians, see Geoffrey J. Giles, ed., *Stunde Null: The End and the Beginning Fifty Years Ago* (Washington, D.C.: German Historical Institute, 1997).

4. Ralf Bentz et al., *Protest! Literatur um 1968. Eine Ausstellung des Deutschen Literaturarchivs in Verbindung mit dem Germanistischen Seminar der Universität Heidelberg und dem Deutschen Rundfunkarchiv im Schiller-Nationalmuseum Marbach am Neckar,* Marbach am Neckar: Deutsche Schillergesellschaft, 1998 (exhibition catalogue).

5. Walter Erhart and Dirk Niefanger, eds., *Zwei Wendezeiten; Blicke auf die deutsche Literatur 1945 und 1989* (Tübingen: Max Niemeyer, 1997).

6. Helmut Kiesel, "Die Restaurationsthese als Problem für die Literaturgeschichtsschreibung," in Erhart and Niefanger, ibid., 13–46.

7. For a very good review of the recent historical literature focusing on the conflict between the forty-fivers and the sixty-eighters and thus on the relation be-

tween the restoration decade and the 1960s, see A. D. Moses, "The Forty-Fivers. A Generation Between Fascism and Democracy," *German Politics and Society* 50 (Spring 1999): 94–126.

8. Kiesel, "Die Restaurationsthese als Problem," 36. No surprise, then, that this account is accompanied in the following essay by Dirk Niefanger by a rather uncritical reading of the *Stunde Null* in plays by Borchert, Zuckmayer, and Weisenborn, or that the *Wende* of 1989–90, which is said to mark the end of post-war literature, is paradigmatically represented by Martin Walser in an essay by Georg Braungart.

9. See Huyssen, In *Twilight Memories*, 37–66.

10. For a critically differentiated view of the literature of the 1960s see Klaus Briegleb, *1968—Literatur in der antiautoritären Bewegung* (Frankfurt am Main: Suhrkamp, 1993); also Klaus Briegleb and Sigrid Weigel, eds., *Gegenwartsliteratur seit 1968* (Munich: Hanser, 1992) (*Hansers Sozialgeschichte der deutschen Literatur*, vol. 12).

11. A parallel attack on the 1960s has been waged in the U.S. culture wars of the late 1980s and 1990s. See Andreas Huyssen, "Palimpsest 1968: USA/Germany," in Ulrich Off and Roman Luckscheiter, eds. *Belles Lettres/Graffiti. Soziale Phantasien und Ausdrucksformen der Achtundsechziger* (Göttingen: Wallstein Verlag, 2001), 37–52.

12. The relevant texts are collected in Deiritz and Krauss. See footnote 1.

13. Frank Schirrmacher, "Abschied von der Literatur der Bundesrepublik," *Frankfurter Allgemeine Zeitung*, October 2, 1990. Reprinted in Deiritz and Krauss, and in Anz, *"Es geht nicht um Christa Wolf"*; see footnote 1.

14. On the limitations of the poststructuralist psychoanalytic trauma discourse that has become so influential in literary and cultural studies, see Dominick LaCapra, *History and Memory after Auschwitz* (Ithaca and London: Cornell University Press, 1998). See also Ruth Leys, *Trauma: A Genealogy* (Chicago and London: Chicago University Press, 2000). The psychoanalytic model may work well when it comes to the individual memory of the survivor or witness, but its application to the public memory of traumatic historical events remains problematic. Neither the thesis of the unrepresentability of trauma, so dominant in the poststructuralist Holocaust discourse in the wake of the important work of Cathy Caruth, nor the moral demand to work through rather than to act out experience (as forcefully posited by LaCapra) seems very useful in analyzing the constitution of public memory. Public memory depends on representations in all its media, and it relentlessly mixes working through and acting out.

15. On the notion of trauma as unresolved experience rooted in history, rather than as something unrepresentable and outside of time, see Ulrich Baer, *Remnants of Song: Trauma and the Experience of Modernity in Charles Baudelaire and Paul Celan* (Stanford, Calif.: Stanford University Press, 2000).

16. Thus several critics have demonstrated that there are a number of other

texts about the topic that Sebald did not acknowledge. But such a critique operates at the same deficient theoretical level as Sebald's own text. As if Foucault had
never written on repression, it assumes that the existence of a large number of
texts proves that there was no repression. Again, repression and discourse are not
mutually exclusive. The empirical critique of Sebald's argument is conceptually
limited, and it misses what Sebald's text actually performs and enacts.

17. W. G. Sebald, *Die Ausgewanderten. Vier lange Erzählungen* (Frankfurt am
Main: Fischer, 1994). American translation: *The Emigrants*, trans. Michael Hulse
(New York: New Directions, 1996).

18. Sigrid Weigel, "Die 'Generation' als symbolische Form. Zum geneaologis-
chen Diskurs im Gedächtnis nach 1945," in *figurationen: gender, literatur, kultur*,
no. 0 (August 2000): 158–73. See also the astute review essay about the recent
wave of historical and sociological literature about generations by A. D. Moses:
"The Forty-Fivers: A Generation Between Fascism and Democracy," *German Politics and Society* 50 (Spring 1999): 94–126.

19. Of great interest here are his multiple rewritings of his book about Stalingrad: Alexander Kluge, *Schlachtbeschreibung*, first ed. Olten and Freiburg, 1964; reworked edition Frankfurt and Hamburg, 1968; expanded new edition Munich,
1978. For a superb analysis of Kluge's writing strategies, see Harro Müller,
"Alexander Kluges analytischer Realismus—Stichworte zu *Schlachtbeschreibung*,"
in *Giftpfeile: Zu Theorie und Literatur der Moderne* (Bielefeld: Aisthesis Verlag,
1994), 221–32.

20. This is not to deny that there were precursors to Holocaust discourse in
the 1950s. But at that time such debates remained more limited to certain group-
ings within the churches or related to cultural products such as the American play
about Anne Frank or Alain Resnais's film documentary *Nuit et Brouillard* (*Night
and Fog*). On the presence of the past in German drama of the early postwar period, see Andreas Huyssen, "Unbewältigte Vergangenheit—unbewältigte Gegenwart," in Reinhold Grimm and Jost Hermand, eds., *Geschichte im Gegenwarts-
drama* (Stuttgart: Kohlhammer Verlag, 1976), 39–53.

21. On the problem of transgenerational traumatization, see Werner Bohleber,
"Das Fortwirken des Nationalsozialismus in der zweiten und dritten Generation
nach Auschwitz," *Babylon* 7 (1990): 70–83.

22. Catastrophe, of course, always lurks not far beneath Stifter's deceptively
harmonious story lines. See Sebald's "Versuch über Stifter," in W. G. Sebald, *Die
Beschreibung eines Unglücks: Zur österreichischen Literatur von Stifter bis Handke*
(Frankfurt am Main: Fischer, 1994), 15–37.

23. W. G. Sebald, *Luftkrieg und Literatur* (Munich: Hanser, 1999), 80.

24. Symptomatic of this view is Ralf Schroeder, "Völlig losgelöst," *Jungle
World* 52:1 (December 2000). Critical but fairer, Dieter Forte, "Menschen werden
zu Herdentieren," *Der Spiegel* (April 7, 1999), or Ingo Arend, "Stufen der Angst,
Freitag 15 (April 9, 1999).

25. Sebald, *Luftkrieg und Literatur*, 20.

26. Erich Nossack, *Der Untergang* (Frankfurt am Main: Suhrkamp, 1963), 43.

27. Ibid., 29ff. I thank Peter Schwartz for the translations from Nossack, Kluge, and Sebald in this chapter.

28. Ibid., 39.

29. Ibid., 73.

30. See, for example, Nossack, ibid., 17.

31. Alexander Kluge, *Neue Geschichten, vols. 1–18 "Unheimlichkeit der Zeit"* (Frankfurt am Main: Suhrkamp, 1977), 9.

32. Ibid., 106.

33. Alexander Kluge and Oskar Negt, *Geschichte und Eigensinn* (Frankfurt am Main: Suhrkamp, 1981), 789.

34. Sebald, *Luftkrieg und Literatur*, 5.

35. W. G. Sebald, *Schwindel. Gefühle* (Frankfurt am Main: Fischer, 1994), 213. English translation: *Vertigo*, trans. Michael Hulse (New York: New Directions, 2000), 187. Translation corrected.

36. W. G. Sebald, "Zwischen Geschichte und Naturgeschichte. Versuch über die literarische Beschreibung totaler Zerstörung mit Anmerkungen zu Kasack, Nossack und Kluge," *Orbis Litterarum* 37 (1982): 345–66.

37. Sebald, *Luftkrieg und Literatur*, 79.

38. Sebald, "Zwischen Geschichte und Naturgeschichte," 362.

39. Ibid., 363.

40. W. G. Sebald, *Austerlitz* (Munich: Hanser, 2001). This last book by Sebald, published shortly before his tragic death, is at the same time his first "real" novel. For a reading of *Austerlitz* as a memory novel see Andreas Huyssen, "The Gray Zones of Remembrance" (forthcoming).